kissing frogs

kissing frogs

HELPING YOUTHS OVERCOME

IMPASSES *and* CHALLENGES

through CUSTOMIZED STORYTELLING

JARED U. BALMER, Ph.D.

Published by Advantage, Charleston, South Carolina.
Member of Advantage Media Group.

ADVANTAGE is a registered trademark and the Advantage colophon is a trademark of Advantage Media Group, Inc.

Printed in the United States of America.

ISBN: 978-1-59932-456-2
LCCN: 2015955301

Advantage Media Group is proud to be a part of the Tree Neutral® program. Tree Neutral offsets the number of trees consumed in the production and printing of this book by taking proactive steps such as planting trees in direct proportion to the number of trees used to print books. To learn more about Tree Neutral, please visit www.treeneutral.com. To learn more about Advantage's commitment to being a responsible steward of the environment, please visit www.advantagefamily.com/green

Advantage Media Group is a publisher of business, self-improvement, and professional development books and online learning. We help entrepreneurs, business leaders, and professionals share their Stories, Passion, and Knowledge to help others Learn & Grow. Do you have a manuscript or book idea that you would like us to consider for publishing? Please visit advantagefamily.com or call 1.866.775.1696.

Acknowledgments

L et me start by thanking my parents, who have long passed way. During my pre-teen years they refused to purchase a TV but instead provided me with a big, fat book—Grimm's Fairy Tales. Those tales filled my head with wonder, something Tom & Jerry would have been incapable off.

Much thanks goes to the late Dr. Margret Hoops, one of my professors at Brigham Young University. She was much more than a teacher. She was a mentor who required top-notch work but provided me with the support and encouragement and the self-belief that I would be capable of doing it.

My gratitude goes to all those gifted women who were involved in the editorial work of this book, namely Heather Bennett, Angela Bulloch, and my beautiful wife, Rosann. They were primarily responsible to translate my "Swinglish" (i.e. English with a Swiss sentence structure) into the King's English.

Last, but not least, I would like to thank the helpful staff of the Advantage Media family who held my hand through the entire process of conveying my thoughts to you, the reader.

foreword

LET ME TELL YOU A STORY…

Take a brief moment to scan your thoughts, emotions, and feelings as you read these six words: *Let me tell you a story.* For most of us, those words take us back to our childhood, or at least a childhood state of being. They transport us to a comfortable, enchanting, and engaging place—a place where challenges are met with the right resources and produce valuable outcomes. The stories that follow tell of successful resolutions to existing challenges and provide guidance, or clues, for successful "storybook endings."

Unfortunately there are times when our children's stories don't end well. Written especially for parents during these times, this book will empower your "editorial skills" in helping your child revise their life stories toward better endings.

I still remember the story of how I first met Jared. It was during the time when the National Association of Therapeutic Schools and Programs (NATSAP) needed some heroes and heroines to take on the challenge of validating their creative approaches to working with children. One of the key figures in championing these efforts was Jared. He was known for his large, visionary prowess and transformative leadership style, which he had demonstrated as founder/CEO at seven residential treatment centers over the last thirty-five years. Possessing a physical stature to match these talents, he cast a formidable presence as he entered a room or discussion. And while Jared certainly is a hero in our story, he utilizes approaches paradoxical to his professional stature. The size that truly matters to him lies in the resources and heroic states within his clients.

As I came to know Jared further, I became much more aware of the clinician side of his work and the thoughtful, kind, and compassionate approaches he took to address the most serious of psychological issues. With this perspective in mind, he creates the scenic backdrop for this book. Being a clinician and parent who utilizes metaphors often, I was eager to discover Jared's "answers" for delivering the perfect metaphor for client change from such a rich source of information. But with an ability to build anticipation and engagement in a way that would make Milton Erickson proud, Jared sets the stage for our acquisition of using metaphors with children by inducting us into his approaches through a backdrop of stories with key embedded elements. To get the most out of the material in the stories, I would encourage you to find a nice, comfortable place to read this part of the book. Allow yourself the full richness of these timeless stories to empower your transderivational search processes to find the best application for these stories. It is only after you have gone through the process of revisiting these stories that you should explore the processes common throughout them.

Most of all, during these stories, look for the times that Jared's experiences and thoughts seem to fit you like a "customized shirt." You know, the type of shirt that not only fits you like a glove but is also tailored to make it feel like a one-in-a-million piece of clothing. This is where Jared's theories, practices, and stories will feel as if he has customized these therapeutic processes specifically for you and your child.

And as distasteful as kissing frogs might be, the story in the epilogue of this book is about a transformed frog from Switzerland who turned into a prince. Over time, through mature examination and thoughtful action, the prince turned into a king. But the measure of this king is not determined by how he rules over others with his vast experience and expertise but rather how he empowers us as parents to be even better with our children and their stories. In this book, a king turns his attention to help the most vulnerable of clients—children—and we, as a profession, are much better because of his work.

Finally, how will you know you are ready to use the gift from the king? When you have the following two conditions: (1) you have decided on the story to tell; and (2) when you say those six words, your child turns to you with sincere and engaging interest: *Let me tell you a story…*

Enjoy the journey!

Michael Gass, PhD, LMFT
Professor, College of Health and Human Services
University of New Hampshire
Durham, New Hampshire

Author of:

- *Adventure Therapy: Theory, Practice, and Research.* NY: Routledge Publishing Company.

- *Effective Leadership in Adventure Programming.* Human Kinetics Publishing, 2nd edition.

- *Reflective Learning: Theory and Practice.* Dubuque, IA: Kendall Hunt Publishing Company.

- *Book of Metaphors: A Descriptive Presentation of Metaphors for Adventure Activities—Volume II.* Dubuque, IA: Kendall Hunt Publishing Company.

- *Adventure Therapy: Therapeutic Applications of Adventure Programming.* Dubuque, IA: Kendall Hunt Publishing Company.

- *Book of Metaphors: A Descriptive Presentation of Metaphors for Adventure Activities.* Durham, NH: University of New Hampshire.

table of contents

introduction

O ne of the highlights of my postdoctoral training was the many hours shared with the late Dr. Milton H. Erickson, a world-famous psychiatrist. He was one of the brilliant minds responsible for the development of *strategic therapy*—a form of short-term psychotherapy that represented a radical departure from traditional psychoanalysis, where a patient would meet with a therapist for months or even years. Strategic therapy was different. Significant change was possible within a few sessions.

A distinctive pattern emerged while I observed Dr. Erickson's work with short-term therapy patients. If a patient asked a question, Dr. Erickson would not answer directly. Instead, he would tell a story drawn from his life experience. It was up to the patient to "extract" the answer from the story. Through this approach, the patient answered his or her own question—with the help of the story. This had a familiar ring to it. Dr. Bruno Bettelheim, a widely known child psychologist, postulated that common fairy tales of the Brothers Grimm had healing properties for children in distress.

In both cases, the challenge was to match the "right" story with the presenting problem. Which story do I pull out of the bag? *Cinderella* or *Sleeping Beauty*? The story of when I broke my arm or the one when I went sailing in San Francisco Bay? Such was my challenge in conducting psychotherapy with children, adolescents, and even adults.

Rather than employing a story from a book, I began experimenting with creating "custom" stories that had a metaphoric connection with the presenting problems of my clients. I learned that "custom" tales were particularly effective with children and adolescents, who often did not jump at the opportunity for change or resented being told what to do. Through storytelling, these clients were no longer focused on me, the authority figure, but sustained their attention by allowing them to identify with the main character. I could see their wheels spinning in an effort to find meaning in what they heard. Moreover, I had their full attention, which is always a great asset when interacting with youths.

This book will take a closer look at the power of the story and proceed to provide systematic instructions to create a customized story—one with therapeutic properties for a specific person who is experiencing a particular impasse or problem. Such stories often have more impact on a person than a lecture, a talking-to, or waving a scolding finger. Indeed, such a story may be a healing gift for a person troubled with an impasse or problem. Stories are powerful.

Give them a try!

CHAPTER 1

the metaphor

This book's purpose is to demonstrate how to teach children through the magic of metaphor. And whether it comes from the entertaining, happily-ever-after fairy tale, the somewhat strange and foreign fable, the profound and stately parable, the inexhaustible allegory, or the ubiquitous saying, the power of metaphor as a learning tool remains preserved within each storytelling format. In the family of language arts, these story types are not-so-distant cousins, bound by common threads. These "genes" have so many shared common features that hearing one makes one think of another. Through these common threads, useful terms emerge, such as *deeper meaning*, *symbolism, figurative devices, similes,* etc. Each of these terms yields greater metaphorical meaning.

By definition, a metaphor is "a figure of speech, in which a term that ordinarily designates an object or idea is used to designate a dissimilar object or idea in order to suggest comparison or analogy, as in the phrase, 'evening of life.'" Thus, any mode of communication that uses comparison to designate ideas or objects qualifies as a metaphor. As in a painting where the meaning is not immediately evident, this art form begs our interpretation.

Naturally, the crafters of folk tales were not the first humans to employ this form of communication. Metaphors have been used since the beginning of time. In fact, the need to compare experiences and capture ideas in word-pictures relates to concepts of space and time and to the development of man. Ancient man, without the use of the alphabet, communicated his experiences metaphorically. Cave paintings all over the world are alive with ancient experiences and impressions. Perhaps the caveman's language could not deliver communication without the picture, and pictures have given rise to the metaphor. In any case, metaphor is as old as man himself. It is part of him; it is innate.

In the modern world, metaphors are the building blocks of any nontechnical text. Their creative and structural uses distinguish good writers from the bad. When Shakespeare's Richard III speaks of "the winter of our discontent," we hear the resonance and truth of the metaphor, the aptness of his choice. On the other hand, an improper or overdone metaphor can be as unwieldy as a five-hundred-pound dumbbell in a steroid-free gym.

In our world, we are inundated with metaphors. They swirl around us and sprout within. We dream in metaphor and go to the psychiatrist to have our metaphors interpreted so that we may discover meaning. Even in our dreams, metaphors remind us of our responsibility to render meaning from our lives. Behavioral scientists have told us that dreams are symbolic representations of our experiences and are reality in disguise—truth dressed up in costume. Whatever the circumstance or nature of our responses, metaphor is powerful. It is enticing, enchanting, and enriching. Metaphor is captivating, engaging, and amusing. Life without it is unthinkable. Its potential for beauty, richness, and power has found application in all ages and cultures.

However, metaphors are not only works of art; they are also literally change agents. They possess the power to stir our souls. They can reach deep inside us and cause us to examine our mind-sets, our attitudes, and our perspectives. Metaphors, properly framed and well timed, can cause us to regroup, to rearrange priorities, to make commitments, and to renew devotions. At times, metaphors shake us up and usually move us in modified directions, and other times they simply fall on us like warm sunshine. But good metaphors always enrich the story, and stories help make us whole by connecting us to one another, as well as ourselves. When using a story to teach a youth, the key is to match the "right" metaphor to the age of the child and his or her perceived problem. A story will explain.

The Story

I was ten years old and in big trouble. The forest next to our home was a favorite playground, where my best friend and I spent hours building forts, whittling branches into weapons, and climbing trees to look out for bad guys. One particular day, we crept into the woods to conceal our contraband. My friend and I had coaxed an older boy into giving us the cigar he proudly produced from his pocket. In our minds, smoking would put us on the fast track to manhood. As we sat down to light up, the secretive nature of the deed only added to our delight.

The consequences of risk-taking are often overlooked in the excitement of such moments. However, my youthful glee was short lived. The problem was due to an unwritten rule in our home, which was, nevertheless, clear to both my brothers and me: No smoking—not ever! My father did not smoke. My mother did not smoke, and Emma Balmer was wise—blessed with a certain motherly clairvoyance. If something was amiss, she knew it. I was sure my mother would eventually get wind of my dalliance, and I would spend the rest of my life in purgatory. This fear sent me into a cascade of thoughts neither remorseful nor apologetic but centered on how I could outsmart my mother and escape her wrath. Finally, it occurred to me that confessing my errant actions with a warmly spoken apology would elicit maternal mercy and stop her from digging further into my business.

Mustering all the courage I possessed, I walked into the kitchen where Mother was preparing a meal. Instinctually, I figured she might be distracted and fail to give me her full attention. Soon, I put on a show of coming clean and acknowledged, in youthful terminology, my gross lack of judgment. When I finished, Mother paused from her work for what seemed like an eternity. I was sure she would give me a licking. What followed was a most perplexing experience: she told me a story.

The Knight of Kardish

Once upon a time, there lived a king and a queen in the small but beautiful kingdom of Kardish. The subjects of the king were peace-loving people. They worked hard on their farms, and the earth was good to them, producing fruits, vegetables, and grains in abundance. Occasionally, the king permitted his people to hunt in the forest—a welcome diversion that brought home more meat and hides for winter warmth. After many years, the neighboring kingdom plundered the small villages on the northern boundary of Kardish, and the king had no choice but to summon his valiant knights to make war against the aggressors.

It was awesome to see the young knights astride their horses. Swords, shields, and armor shone in the sun. Onlookers waved in delight as the procession passed. In one of the castle windows stood a young man not quite old enough to join the campaign, wishing for his chance to fight. At first, battle was just a dream. However, as the war continued, more knights were required. The king summoned the young man, telling him his skills were crucial to saving the kingdom. He knighted the lad and said, "I have taught you well, and I trust you. Make haste to the battlefield; your fellow knights need you tomorrow."

The young knight wasted no time. He spent his whole evening in preparation—polishing his shield, brushing his horse, sharpening his sword, and giving last-minute instructions to his page. With the first crow of the rooster, the young knight set off. He was proud. He had waited long for the moment to prove his worth. The opportunity to test his skills in battle was a dream come true.

The young knight, mounted on his big white horse, followed the road north along a wide river, crossed that river and several more, and then rode up a mountain to the edge of a great forest.

Suddenly, a knight covered in black armor and riding a large black horse emerged from the trees. "I see you are on your way to the great conflict. Don't you think it would be good to test your skills with me before you go into battle?" he said.

The young knight hesitated. His page reminded him that fellow knights needed his help and awaited his arrival. Alas, regretfully, the young knight could not pass up this chance for a fight. He lowered the visor on his helmet, moved his long wooden boom to a horizontal position, and challenged the other knight to a jousting match.

Both contestants fought long and hard. As the jousting continued, the page's words rang in the young knight's ears. "What am I doing here?" he finally asked himself. "I know I am needed on the battlefield." Quickly turning his horse around, the young knight raced toward his destiny.

When he arrived at the battlefield, he discovered that the conflict had been won without him. His prowess had never been tested in a true battle. He joined his fellow knights, and all together they headed toward home, singing about their victory.

Back at the castle, the young knight reported to the king. "I did not go directly to the battle to join up with the other knights. Instead, I stopped along the way to take on a black knight in a jousting match," he confessed. The young man anxiously awaited the king's reply.

"Ha-ha-ha," the king laughed. "You have told me a very funny story, but I know better. I know you did what I trusted you to do. You wouldn't stop along the way and waste your time on a meaningless match."

The young knight was puzzled. He had expected the king to rebuke him, but instead, the king merely continued in a serious tone.

"And even if you did postpone your journey to battle the black knight, my belief in you cannot be broken. That is the sacred law of trust among the knights of the kingdom of Kardish."

At this point in the story, my mother looked straight into my eyes and finished the story.

The young knight left the castle a happy but thoughtfully humble boy. He grew up to be a fierce and loyal warrior who always tried to do his best. Years later, after he had experienced many things, his understanding grew. He became a lord within the land. He was respected by all and lived happily ever after.

Mother kissed me on the head and returned to her cooking. I was baffled. She offered no reprimand or angry accusation. Her words carried no hint of sarcasm, criticism, or disappointment. Not once did she shake her finger at me. *A story? And, for heaven's sake, not even a story about smoking!* Perhaps my mother was beginning to lose her edge. In spite of my trepidation, it appeared I was off the hook. I remember backing out of the kitchen and watching her as she continued to work. Then I quickly turned, ran out the door, and raced down the street to play. The story was far from my mind.

When I knew it was time for dinner, I started home again. As I walked along the edge of the forest, I thought I saw something lingering in the darkness of the trees and imagined the black knight on his journey. The story began to weigh heavily on my mind. My mother never wasted words. She was the practical, down-to-earth matron of our home.

At last, I realized she was trying to teach me something.

The Practicality of Visualization and the Power of Thought

There was little question that I was the young knight. I had wanted to prove to myself (and others) how cool I was—a ten-year-old with the daring of a man. My counterpart was also young, with a misdirected craving for adventure. We were soul mates, he and I. Conclusions of our misadventure rolled in and out of my mind over the course of many weeks.

Sometimes days went by when I did not think of the story. Then something would spark a memory, and my "friend" would appear. I could see his shining armor and his proud stature, and I could picture myself in much the same way. One time I wondered how someone so heroic could have messed up the opportunity to prove himself. Wait a minute—was I thinking about him, or was I asking myself this question? We had both broken trust with those who loved us, but I knew the end of his story, how the knight quickly saw the error of his ways and understood that trust is a precious commodity. As he grew and matured, the knight was able to move past his childish mistakes to become a pretty good guy. Over the course of my life, I often saw him as a mentor when I needed to see the errors of my ways.

The king's relationship to the young knight resembled the relationship I had with my parents. I knew both my father and my mother were a mix of authority and warmth. They felt a responsibility to protect the kingdom in which I lived and to teach me character-building principles. The king loved the young knight. My parents loved me. Both the young knight and I had blown it. However, in the shame of letting others down, I gained awareness that my behavior wasn't a death sentence. It was a learning experience. Through the words of the king, my mother implied she would *never* not trust me again. Her faith gave me hope.

Unfortunately, I took many more opportunities to raise hell while I was growing up. I had always known it was a breach of family rules to take up smoking, but in my ten-year-old mind, this experiment was a momentary hiccup, free of long-term impact. In later years, I continued to justify trouble-making and rule-breaking as temporary insanity, but each time I faced a choice, and that pesky black knight came into my head. He was my alter ego, not evil but certainly dangerous. I thought of him as my oppositional force, my distraction, and a devil on my shoulder. His presence forced me to consider the consequences of my decisions. In time, I came to understand that even small infractions could lead to great deviations in character.

In the immediate days and weeks following my brief smoke, mother's story puzzled and frustrated me. It burrowed into my brain, challenged my so-called reality, and exposed my skewed thinking. Once the initial confusion had passed, I began a rumination process that peeled away layers of realization and enlightenment: (1) I had misused my mother's trust; (2) she cared for me and would never give up on me; and (3) in the end, she knew I would turn out all right. The story kept growing, developing, and refreshing itself as I found new ways to process the information it contained. The lessons were profound.

"Why?" Is an Excellent Question

The brain of a child is like a dry sponge, sucking up the water of story and experience. Even young children are capable of connecting ideas to actions. As they mature, their ability to process complex information and form more meaningful conclusions grows within them. Children seek information as if life depends on it (and sometimes it does). They stubbornly avoid going to bed because they fear missing something important. "Why?" rolls off their tongues with maddening frequency. Often, a straightforward answer is all they require—more facts to hang in the brain, more information to help them connect the dots. It is important to emphasize, however, that the best time for children to absorb the answers to their ever-present questions is when they want to figure things out, not when they are being lectured. The trick is to recognize when a child might benefit from a *thinking session*. In those moments, the right story could be a riveting pathway to greater understanding, moral awareness, and even the power to improve lives.

Storytelling can be a tremendous tool in the hands of a parent. In later chapters, we will explore a range of storytelling styles and strategies. It is important to add that all metaphors invite children to switch on their imaginations. If children see themselves in a story, the messages gained can become deeply personal, impacting each in the here and now as well as helping to shape future behaviors.

Unlocking the Magic of Metaphor

When we discuss the power of story, we're really talking about the relevance and depth of its metaphors. So what is a metaphor exactly?

It's a linguistic trick that creates unexpected connections between one thing and another: *a mighty fortress is our God; they were drowning in a sea of debt; she is the light of my life.*

Each of these examples paints an emotionally laden picture in the human mind that intensifies memory and reinforces an understanding of the message: God is as an impenetrable, protective force for those who seek shelter; a couple struggles to breathe in a neck-deep pile of bills and demands; a beloved's face glows with hope and promise. Metaphoric messages hook listeners into making emotional investments. Fairy tales, fables, parables, and allegories (stories in which every character and event is part of an extended metaphor) are proven methods for conveying important lessons.

Think of the last formal lecture you attended. Are you able to recall its content in any detail? Not likely or perhaps only vaguely. However, if the speaker chose to illustrate a critical point with a story or metaphoric narrative, the chances are much better that you will remember the points. During a grinding lecture, a story drafts up like a breath of fresh air. Through the magic of metaphor, teachers across the ages have opened windows for listeners to escape the restrictions of syntax, logic, and reason. While the general text of a lecture is quickly forgotten, a story and its message live on in memory. Symbolic stories, or metaphors, are like superglue on the brain.

Why Metaphor Works

Metaphor works in a variety of ways and for many reasons. Three following elements will serve as an introduction.

1. *Telling a story calms the waters.*

Our lives are stressful, conflict is inevitable, and we live in a contentious world. Therefore, civil discourse must begin at home.

In making the choice to relate a story instead of delivering a reprimand, my mother avoided confrontation. I came to the kitchen prepared for an argument. I think I wanted a standoff—a forum in which to vent about silly family rules, thus proving I was more a man than my mother thought. Her story defused a volatile moment, deprived me of playing the antagonist, and left me nothing with which *to* argue.

We learn best if we are at ease and relatively relaxed. Very little change is produced by a steady dose of stern, finger-wagging lectures. An overly anxious person can't process new information, because he or she is preoccupied or exhausted by stress. Thus, a *student* is most receptive to new information in a state of calm, free from external or internal conflict.

2. *Metaphoric connections are personal.*

Transformative learning takes place only when an individual finds a way to school herself. Metaphors permit us to generalize from specifics—to take general information and find specific applications for it. What we experience in one setting is often interpreted and applied in another situation—if we think metaphorically.

Watching a squirrel gather nuts and store them in his hideaway, for example, may stimulate our thinking—and possibly change behaviors. When we subsequently learn about an impending snowstorm, we may be prompted to visit the grocery store and purchase food for the next few days. Observing how a young girl reacts when she gets the cold shoulder from her schoolmates may influence the way we relate to friends and strangers at our next social gathering.

The metaphor precipitates learning by providing a shortcut to some essential connection—a connection made from one's own experience. Free of scientific analysis, philosophical discussion, or explicit explanation, a story invites the listener to participate in a self-made experience.

3. Learning happens in the time frame of the listener.

Each listener picks up the informational threads in a narrative at his own leisure—beckoned but not compelled to come along on a story's journey. For a variety of reasons, an individual may catch the first train of understanding or wait for later transportation—be it car, bus, or ferry. Each listener is in charge of getting to that pivotal juncture known as the "ah hah!" moment, the epiphany or denouement when everything becomes clear. Some may get there immediately. Others start with a great deal of pondering and sometimes tuck the metaphor away in the brain for future use. You will recall that for many hours I simply forgot about my mother's story. In the moment I passed through the forest, something sparked a memory of that young knight in the kingdom of Kardish, and it was at that moment that I discovered the story's metaphor.

In the fifty-plus years since I heard my mother's first story, I've confronted more than a few knights on black horses. That image from my childhood has surfaced many times as a reminder to stay the course. As a marriage and family therapist, who has dedicated his professional experience to working with children and adolescents, I have often used the power of metaphor to encourage change in the lives of my clients and their families.

Let me invite you to remain with me, for I have another story to tell.

CHAPTER 2

old is new

The previous chapter addressed the power and magic of the metaphor. We discovered what a fabulous teaching tool it can be, particularly for parenting children. In this chapter, you will become more familiar with the historical perspective of metaphors. An "archeological dig" into the subject will further underline the ingenious approach of metaphors in inspiring and helping children overcome impasses and crises. Of course, this is not a new idea but an old one. Unfortunately, the practice of storytelling has largely been pushed to the background by the rise in electronics, which can never take the place of one's personal imagination—key features of story.

Fairy tales can magically impact children. The story, like the mythic fairy tale, beckons the child to abandon rules and the harshness of reality and enter a world where make-believe reigns. This world offers an expanse of freedom and limitless travels into the past and future through geographical and conceptual realms. Such worlds allow one to escape the pressures of everyday reality, yet the fairy tale provides its own construct of order. There are rules in this magical kingdom: rules about morals, decency, promises, and commitment. The fairy tale does not diminish or abandon reality for a bizarre, psychotic-like world—a world similar to (though more exotic than) the real world, using well-defined parameters of human dignity and propriety. The story allows us to lose touch with the physical or material in the here and now and urges us in a subtle, persuasive way to reexamine our values and rediscover what we treasure. Such imaginative examination is the material that, in turn, creates everyday reality.

Tales and Stories

In the beloved old European tales, retold by the Grimm Brothers, the fairy tale provides a template—a compass or sorts, whereby hopes and dreams can be transformed into reality. Generally, these stories follow an *archetypical* theme. Within the inherent theme, the hero is faced with a dilemma. The dilemma may represent fears, angst, or obstacles of the human condition. However, the theme provides an escape and offers a resolution. The escape from the dilemma may come about by external or internal means but only after the hero makes a personal effort, sacrifice, or willingness to risk.

Behavioral scientists suggest that stories hold therapeutic value because of their archetypical themes. They represent a form of recognizing angst and provide hope and eventual victory in a growing, developing way.

The Grimms' tale, *The Valiant Little Tailor*, is a classic example of this type of story impact:

A little tailor is enticed by a woman who sells jam, but he does not purchase enough to make the woman happy. She leaves disgruntled. However, the tailor likes the jam and believes it will make him stronger and more cunning. He spreads some on a slab of bread. Soon a swarm of flies appear. With rage, he manages to kill seven flies in one strike. Overcome with pride, he takes a leather belt and carves the words "seven in one blow." His pride does not stop there; he wants the whole world to know of his feat. Preparing for his journey, he packs a bit of old cheese before setting off.

Outside he notices a bird caught in the bushes and puts it in the pack with the cheese. Now, he is happily on his way. As he reaches the top of a mountain range, he runs into a terrible giant. Bravely, the little tailor approaches the beast and asks him to join him to see the world and to seek his fortune. The giant looks at the tailor contemptuously and calls him a rascal and a miserable fellow. The tailor responds by taking off his coat and displaying his belt with the words "seven in one blow." The giant, believing the tailor killed seven men with one blow, now shows more respect for the tailor.

Wanting some reassurance about the tailor's strength, the giant picks up a rock and squeezes it so hard that water drops out of the stone. "Can you do that?" the giant asks. The tailor counters by pulling out his old cheese. He squeezes it so hard that whey spills out of it. The giant can't believe it. He takes a rock and throws it so high in the air that it nearly vanishes. The tailor responds by throwing the bird into the air until it vanishes from view.

The giant is impressed but wants to test the tailor further. He asks the tailor to help him carry a big oak tree that has fallen to ground in the woods. The tailor suggests the giant carry the trunk and roots while he carries the branches and leaves, insisting that his task is more difficult. As the giant picks up the tree, the tailor jumps on the branches and sings a song. The giant, unable to look back, soon gets tired and lets the tree down and the tailor quickly jumps off.

They walk farther, and the giant pulls down some branches of a cherry tree and asks the tailor to hold on to the branches. The tailor does so and is hurled into the air as the branches snap back. Confused, the giant asks why he does not have enough strength to hold the branches down, and the tailor responds that he purposely jumped over the tree to avoid bullets from nearby hunters. The tailor challenges the giant to jump over the tree, but he is unable to do so and lands in the crown of the tree.

The giant invites the tailor to sleep at his house for the night and offers him his own bed. At midnight, the giant awakens and splits the bed in half with a giant axe, hoping to kill the little tailor. But the tailor, finding the bed too large for his small frame, had curled up in a corner and escapes the attempt.

The next day, the tailor marches on and eventually finds himself in the courtyard of a king's palace. There, overcome with fatigue, he falls asleep. While sleeping, passersby notice the words on his belt:

"seven with one blow." Thinking the tailor a great warrior, they tell the king, who quickly enlists him into his army. The king privies special housing for the little tailor, and the other soldiers become jealous and want to get rid of him. However, they are afraid to kill the tailor, thinking he could take down seven soldiers with one blow. Instead, they ask the king for discharge, hoping the king will release the little tailor and not rid the kingdom of all soldiers.

As suspected, the king doesn't want to lose his army but does not dare to dismiss the little tailor for fear he may kill the king's people and place himself on the throne. The king hatches a plan. He asks the tailor to slay two giants that live in a nearby wood, who have damaged, robbed, and murdered townspeople. If successful, the king promises the tailor his only daughter in marriage and half of his kingdom.

The tailor sets off into the woods as one hundred horsemen follow. At the edge of the forest, the tailor tells the horsemen to remain as he ventures on. Soon, he finds the two giants asleep under a tree. The tailor fills his pockets with stones, climbs the tree, and periodically lets a stone fall on the chest of one of the giants. Eventually, this giant wakes up and insists that his companion stop hitting him in the chest. The other giant denies the act, and both fall asleep again.

Now the tailor throws rocks at the chest of the other giant. Again, they grumble at each other and eventually fall back asleep. The tailor starts his game anew. This time, the giants become furious at each other, rip out entire trees, and clobber each other to death. The tailor jumps from his tree and with his sword gives each giant a few hacks in the breast before returning to the horsemen.

In disbelief, the horsemen inspect the dead giants. "Only a man who is able to kill seven in one blow can do such a thing," they say.

The little tailor wants to claim his reward, but the king demands one more heroic task. The tailor is asked to capture a unicorn that does great damage to the kingdom. "A small task for the man who can kill seven with one blow!" proclaims the tailor. With axe and rope, he sets off into the forest with additional attendees. Together, they wait.

Deep in the forest, the unicorn rushes the tailor in ambush, who quickly hides behind a tree before the unicorn rams his horn directly into it. The tailor places a rope around the unicorn's neck and frees it from the tree with his axe. Soon, the little tailor arrives at the king's castle with the unicorn in tow.

Again, the king forgoes his promise and demands a third heroic task. This time the tailor must capture a wild boar that has done great damage in the wood. The wild boar runs after the tailor, who flees into a nearby chapel and lures the boar within. The tailor quickly locks the front door and jumps out of a window, capturing the boar.

The king finally makes good on his promises, and the tailor marries his daughter and is given half of the kingdom. When the daughter learns that the clever giant-killer is nothing more than a very clever little tailor, the king plans to put him in chains and send him way. As the soldiers outside the tailor's bedroom make ready to bind him, the little tailor says, "I have slain seven in one blow, killed

two giants, caught a unicorn, and taken a wild boar. Should I be
afraid of those who are standing outside my door?"

When the soldiers hear the tailor's words, a great fear seizes them.
The men flee, and the little tailor becomes king.

The story of the little tailor is an example of how fairy tales help
us recognize unconscious fears and concerns, while simultaneously
offering solutions to such dilemmas. Of course, solutions are not
presented to the listener on a silver platter. For this very reason, fairy
tales are often referred to as riddles in some countries. The label
"riddle" immediately challenges the listener to hunt for a hidden
message or lesson. Such a lesson, if discovered, holds the therapeutic
keys to unlock doors and gain newfound knowledge and insight.

Fairy tales reveal the basic issues confronting humankind: good
and evil, life and death, intrigue and manipulation, weakness and
strength, moral propriety and ungovernable lust.

In the case of *Hansel and Gretel*, story characters find themselves
confronted with the unpredictable, life-threatening forest. Behind
every tree lurks a new danger. A theme of basic survival, the most
powerful of all human drives, is depicted through hunger—which
provides the story line. The struggling woodcutter and his wife,
unable or unwilling to feed four mouths, opt for their own survival
and hatch a cunning plan to "lose" their children in the labyrinth of
the deep, dark forest. Ironically, the children find a house made of the
most enticing food for any child: candy. But instead of satisfying their
hunger and offering them nutrition, the evil witch attempts to turn
the children into fattened pigs. The children have become the means
to survive evil, as they must face death. Confronted with despair,

Hansel and Gretel reach deep into their inner bags of resources. Through innovation and courage, they deceive death, defeat evil, and live happily ever after.

Snow White, along with the Seven Dwarfs, experiences the jealousy of an evil stepmother, who is envious of her stepdaughter's youth and beauty. The betrayed Snow White is brought back to life by the very elements the evil stepmother attempted to destroy: her youth, her love, and her beauty. Only true love brings her back to life.

Translating human emotions and inner experience into a visual depiction of human interaction is the true magic of the fairy tale. It clothes the abstract concept so that it can be recognized. The tale becomes the wrapping around the invisible man, revealing to us where he really is, thus giving us an indication of his true shape and form.

This symbolism is perhaps nowhere as sharply depicted as in the familiar tale of *The Frog Prince*. In this story, the princess loses her most precious treasure in the abyss of the well. She cannot retrieve this worldly treasure on her own. Faced with losing it forever, she enlists the aid of the most repulsive creature, a frog. Now she is forced, through her promise, to manifest affection for an ugly, slimy frog. The reward for overcoming selfishness, keeping one's word, and for showing affection for the despised and the repugnant brings the princess her treasure and the ultimate reward for any princess: a prince. Happiness. The good life. Someone to love and be loved by— the very essence of life. The message delivered to the young listener through the story is an important one: the acquisition of goods is a far cry from what brings us true happiness—love.

Common Elements

Do such tales carry common themes? Is there a collective thread that runs through each of these stories? Initially, this doesn't seem to be the case, because the main characters are as diverse as life itself. The clever tailor seems unrelated to the forgotten child; the aggressive character shows no comparison to the patiently enduring virgin. The discrepancies are apparent in the poor servant and the rich king, the humble herdsman and the powerful emperor, and in the beautiful young girl and the beastly old man.

These characters represent the wide spectrum of human life. On closer examination, however, they represent something deeper. In reality, the humble, despised servant ends up living in a castle, and the beastly old man turns out to be a prince. The starving children end up never worrying about food, and the ugly, slimy frog turns into a handsome young man. The "dummy" turns out to be most clever. The one shrouded in ugliness transforms herself into beauty. The weak and crippled exchange a deficit for power and strength. In the magic wonderland of the fairy tale, all things are possible. Every pauper can become a prince.

The message is clear: a *nobody* can become *somebody*.

But is this a horrible oversimplification? Is the fairy tale telling us that we can cheat reality and through some hocus-pocus become wealthy, beautiful, young, and wise? Is the tale a cheap literary drug that allows us to forget the mundane of our existence? Or does the story plant the seed of an idea, the beginning of inspiration?

Indeed, fairy tales represent the hope or reassurance that man can overcome adversity, transform, mature, develop, and master the seemingly unattainable. The fairy tale is symbolic of the struggles and aspirations of all children, and for that matter, all of us as we seek to acquire our own "kingdom" within. We all want a place we can govern. Not in the political sense as in controlling property and people, but we all long for mastery of the inner self. The crown of the fairy prince is the crown of achieving selfhood. The acquisition of wealth is not of money but of a *rich* life. The shedding of the frog-like appearance is the surrendering of what is undesirable within us and a celebration of that which is true and beautiful.

You Have to Work for It

Great fairy tales do not convey the notion that achievements come easily. In fact, most classic fairy tales depict a struggle, a fight, and a difficult problem to overcome. The heroes are people who operate on their own. Without much deviation, the main character of the story, time and time again, faces major obstacles—which he or she must confront. More significantly, our idol is not usually equipped with magical powers.

The hero is one who ventures out into the world to find fortune. This character separates himself or herself from familiar social boundaries and relationships and has no special endowments, but by doing the right thing, he or she finds a solution. The "right thing" for Hansel and Gretel is to not to give up but to relentlessly search for a solution. Being patient and embracing the primitive life turns the key for Snow White. The appearance of the fairy godmother in *Cinderella* embodies the notion of having the courage to admit, "I am stuck."

Perhaps the most important element of all is the fact that the outcome of a fairy tale goes far beyond the expectation of the hero.

One does not just return home safe and sound; he or she returns with riches. The person who once left in shame now returns with honor. The humble returns with power. The *nobody* becomes somebody and marries into nobility. The princess retrieves her golden ball, and the frog becomes the real reward. The reward exceeds heroes' expectations, thus teaching the invaluable lesson that overcoming adversity ultimately bestows unexpected rewards.

For centuries, the elite have disregarded fairy tales, yet many of the great poets permitted themselves to be inspired by them. Among children and the common folk, fairy tales have always found willing recipients. Tales are still being told in children's bedrooms all over the globe, engendering hope, encouragement, and self-esteem. Every young listener mirrors himself or herself as the hero of the story, vicariously experiencing the anguish of the impending doom—and eventually basking in the glory of having prevailed.

Little has changed over the centuries. Whether the story is told by Mom or Dad, Grandma, Grandpa, or viewed on the movie screen, fairy tales are as beloved today as they were when they were first told.

Just ask a child.

CHAPTER 3

some more archaeology

The previous chapter discussed the enduring treasure of fairy tales to answer why these types of stories have persisted throughout the ages. And for the purpose of this book, we identified imaginative affects upon the individual receiving the fairy tale. This chapter will undertake the discovery of a few very important cousins to the fairy tale and solidify our understanding of the power of metaphor as a learning and problem-solving tool.

The Parable

Nothing has contributed so extensively to the shaping of ethics and morality than religious beliefs. Laws of nations, states, and communities are based on humankind's relationship to deities. The writings of Mohammed, Buddha, and Jesus continue to have broad, contemporary applications.

Some years ago on a London subway wall, a dirty, partially torn poster caught my attention. The upper half of the poster depicted a picture of Jesus. Written beneath was an interesting observation that said: *He never wrote a book. He never held a public office. He never owned his own house. He never traveled farther than a few dozen miles from home. His executioners were hoping his ideas would die along with him at his public killing, yet he influenced, and will continue to do so, hundreds of millions of people every day.*

The statement is impressive to believers and nonbelievers, alike. But how did Jesus do it? How did he and other moral and religious teachers accomplish such feats? The answer is simple—by telling stories. Simple stories. A story we recognize as *parable*. For example, Jesus told of a sower, sowing seeds. Some of these seeds fell onto unfertile soil and died. Others fell in shallow soil, and the weak root structure would not support the plant. Some seeds fell on stony ground and were torched by the sun, while others fell on fertile ground, sprouted, and grew into mature plants that bore fruit.

While the use of stories in the instructions of moral principle is by no means unique to Jesus, no one used the parable as exclusively as the New Testament rabbi did. In fact, some of the Gospel authors indicate that "without a parable, spake he not unto them." It is rather interesting to discover that the actual words uttered by Christ make up a remarkably small portion of the New Testament text. The majority of that text consists of parables.

Before the Gutenberg press, oral tradition and handwritten texts preserved Jesus's parables. The stories were time-release capsules that allowed people the extraordinary opportunity to think, providing even the greatest minds with puzzlement and challenge. In the halls of higher institutions of learning and in every Sunday school class, attempts are made to render meaning from those plain stories. The wonderment is nothing new. Even the disciples of Jesus were bewildered by his parables.

Following Jesus's telling of the parable of the sower, the disciples "came, and said unto him, 'Why speakest though unto them in parables?'" In the classic teaching traditions of the rabbi, Jesus did not answer them directly but answered the question with another parable—a story. In fact, he used eight different parables to explain the meaning of the first.

The great teacher was determined not to provide his listeners with a direct answer but to provide a discovery process of what the meaning may be. The meaning is hidden or veiled for those "who [have] eyes to see and ears to hear." Through this process, the parable waxes powerful. Depending on the interpreter, the same story can have multiple applications. Influenced by varying levels of maturity, knowledge, enlightenment, and stages or forms of belief, each parable takes on a different form in the mind of its receiver. Whether there are single or multiple interpretations, the meanings are derived by paying close attention to the setting and context in which the story is told. Regardless of singular or multiple meanings, the applications of each of these simple stories are as numerous as their listeners.

In the parable of the Good Samaritan, a Jew traveling from Jerusalem to Jericho is attacked and mugged by bandits. Lying on the wayside, the man is left for dead. The unfortunate traveler is ignored by "a certain priest" and a Levite. However, the mugged Jew is rescued by a Samaritan (Samaritans were considered to be of lesser status than the Jews). The rescuer not only administers first aid to the victim but also transports him to an inn to recover. There, the Samaritan deposits some money with the innkeeper so that proper medical care can be provided. Before leaving, he offers instructions with the innkeeper to let him know if the money should prove insufficient.

The applications derived from this simple story are manifold. A young child might conclude that one should never travel alone. Another person may decide that one should always be ready to render help. To another listener, the story may suggest that one ought not to be prejudiced toward others. And to yet another person, the parable may point out that when someone is in need, simple aid is not enough—and assistance for a full recovery is essential. These are but a few interpretations, but in truth, any thoughtful application is, in fact, the right application. Whatever the individual finds in the search for meaning *is* truth.

In the parable of the talents, the master entrusts three of his servants with $2,000, $5,000, and $1,000, respectively. The master, leaving for a trip, hopes all three servants invest their money wisely. The first two servants do so by doubling their initial endowment. The third servant, however, buries his money in the ground for fear of investing it badly and, thereby, losing it. When the master returns, he praises the first two servants and reprimands the other, demanding that his portion, $1,000, be given to the first servant. The master counsels the servant, adding that he who does not put his money to work will lose the resources he has—to one who is putting his own to work.

Every banker will certainly echo the message of the parable, that money is placed best where it can be put to work. The Hollywood talent agent is reaffirmed in his belief that a talent is wasted if it is not exercised and applied. The sociologist concludes that it does not matter what your socio-economic status is but what you do to improve it. The business manager reads it to mean that you better put your assets to work or you will inevitably lose those you already have.

The applications from such stories are innumerable. It is in the diverse application that we find the power and magnificence of this simple story form. The parable does not force the issue; it does not tell the reader how he must apply the meaning but lets him make that judgment. Not only does the reader discover its applications, but every re-reading also unveils new ones. Because of this ongoing process, it's easy to understand why parables never die.

The Allegory

Allegory possesses many of the properties of fairy tales and parables. This form possesses similar story-like qualities but makes no overt attempt to teach moral principles. Yet, it is more than these forms combined. A true allegory is a work of art, a complete, self-standing whole in which deeper meanings underlie literal meanings. The fairy tale seeks to entertain first, while the parable clearly aims to teach moral or religious reasoning. The allegory is capable of both and perhaps more. This form presents a greater element—a lasting message under the guise of another.

Many famous allegories are attributed to the ancient Greek writer, Aesop, and perhaps his best-known story is that of *The Fox and the Grapes*. On the surface (its literal level of meaning), the story tells of a fox that wants a bunch of grapes that are hanging high above his head. He desperately tries to reach at them but eventually gives up, saying that the grapes are sour anyway. Philosophers, mothers, fathers, and students of human behavior have interpreted the allegorical meaning of this simple story in many different and profound ways. Most of them share the common element that the ego of man does not allow him to accept defeat but ascribes blame or cause for underachievement outside of the self.

In the tragic opera of *Faust* by Charles Gounod, the main character, an old German philosopher, desperately wants his youth back. In other literary versions of the same story, Faust desires divine-like powers. He wants to know all human experiences and have the power to do anything. He meets Mephistopheles, the Devil, who offers him a deal. If he will sell his soul to the Devil, Faust may enjoy all that he wishes. Of course, when the time arrives for Faust to enter the Devil's domain, he has second thoughts and desperately wants to repent, but it is too late. The Devil takes him away. Allegorical implications are abundant. Some men want to be like God, having power over aging, wanting to remain young forever. Some want money to buy anything or seek power and influence over their fellow men. In the process, they are willing to do whatever it takes to get there. They are willing to make any sacrifice—even selling themselves at the peril of their own moral destruction and death.

This message is not so different from the well-known story of *Moby Dick* by Herman Melville. Ahab, the captain of the whaling ship *Pequod* sets out to hunt the fierce white whale known as Moby Dick. Ahab is well acquainted with Moby Dick. In a previous hunt for the whale, the captain lost a leg. Now he hunts Moby Dick through all seven seas. Allegorically, however, the story has many deeper and hidden meanings. Some have suggested that the whale represents the wild, mysterious, and complex forces operating upon our lives. Others feel that Captain Ahab may be symbolic of man's heroic struggle to subdue these mysterious forces. There are those men and women who pursue the "white whales" of their minds, only to find that an unrestrained obsession with the hunt may be self-defeating.

Expounding on the three described allegories, one can certainly become philosophical, but allegories need not be laden with philosophical ballast. One can turn almost every story into an allegory. Cervantes's magnificent and ever-amusing tall tale of *Don Quixote* and his windmills is a perfect example. Being a literary genius is not required to discover a story behind the story. Most of us have fought windmills in our own minds. The struggle can be a psychotic-like episode. When we are engaged in fighting ideological windmills, the task sometimes invites the ridicule of many and the admiration of few. Often, the passing of time is required to discover the genius behind the "crazy" idea. Histories of Quixote are rich, though there are few. History at large is rich with allegories. Many of our experiences serve as allegories of events yet to come.

Sayings

All teenagers I have ever spoken with complain about a repertoire of sayings thrown at them by their parents. The practice begins with, "Early to bed, early to rise, makes a man healthy, wealthy, and wise," and, "The early bird catches the worm," and graduates to, "An apple a day keeps the doctor away." They say there is a saying for every occasion, time of day, or circumstance, and yes, these parents are probably right.

Sayings are an integral part of every culture. In fact, the sayings of one's culture are often quoted by other cultures. I have always wondered whether Confucius really said all those things. Regardless, sayings are a staple of oral and written tradition. Without them, communication would be impoverished. Not only are sayings the spice of speakers, but they have also traditionally been important teaching tools. In using them, we are allowed to say something to somebody without coming right out and saying it. We want to avoid the shock of dropping directly in through the front door but rather sneak in quietly through the back door.

Sayings provide a polite way of being critical, an indirect way of teaching something, and a covert way of getting a point across. Utilizing sayings is an implicit way of telling a person what you think and making them *think* in the process. Sayings are so important that we measure a person's intelligence quotient (IQ) by an ability to interpret a saying correctly. *Shallow brooks are noisy; rolling stones gather no moss;* and *let sleeping dogs lie* are some of the sayings for interpretation among recipients in standardized intelligence tests.

In spite of a teenager's disregard for such sayings, each has the magical power of making lasting impressions. Most adults have no trouble recalling the sayings they heard as youngsters from their own parents. Why do sayings stick? We remember them for the same reason we remember those fairy tales Mother told us and the parables we heard in Sunday school. We remember them because they have the same properties as the allegory or the fable. We remember them because they require us to be participants in discovering the message behind the message. Thus, the message belongs to the receiver as much as it belongs to the sender. When we must discover and employ our own meanings, we have a greater propensity to take ownership in the project of living.

CHAPTER 4

the science of metaphor: turning stories into therapy

In the previous chapters, the power and far-reaching implications of fairy tales, metaphors, allegories, sayings, fables, and parables were discussed. Metaphors and related concepts are often acknowledged for how they influence and affect us, but frequently they are not recognized for *how* and *why* they work from a technical perspective.

This chapter discusses the fundamental workings of the metaphor and will assist in answering the question: *How* does the magic work? This chapter will show how the fairy tale, the story, and the parable hold therapeutic value that benefits youth who experience an impasse due to a host of possible problems, including learning, behavioral, confidence, and other issues.

Scanning for a Fit

The most salient feature of the metaphor is the process that some scientists have referred to as the *transderivational search*, first articulated by Bandler and Grinder (1976). The term denotes an inquiry of sorts and is a rather complicated and unclear process that occurs within the cerebral cortex, whereby the brain attaches meaning to experiences by sorting and categorizing information into a meaningful whole. It is the brain's way of scanning through heaps of information, focusing on specific pieces, while discarding others. This complicated search can be explained by a rather crude analogy of the familiar children's toy—the pegboard.

The pegboard is usually a rectangular piece of wood or plastic with a number of geometric shapes cut out. The child is presented with the task of fitting several geometric pieces into their corresponding place on the pegboard. For a three-year-old, this may be a piece of cake; however, a one-year-old may struggle for hours as he or she tries to fit the triangle into the rectangular space, the circle into the square shape, or the octagon into the circular hole.

The basic version of the pegboard establishes that an equal number of holes and pieces are present to fit each hole. A more advanced version may have more pieces than appropriate slots, so that certain blocks are left over and disregarded after all the slots have been appropriately filled.

The Pegboard

Think of the pegboard as the brain of the child and the different shapes as information presented to the brain. The pegboard, or the brain, holds the sum of an individual's experiences. Of course, the child's total experiences are never static, as ongoing experiences continually expand the pegboard. Thus, the brain of the developing child allows the youth to interpret events with increasing complexity.

This process is unique to a particular child, as no two children have exactly the same life experiences. Therefore, the ever-growing collection of experiences, and the conclusions one draws from them, renders each with a truly unique pegboard. Some individuals may have similar or identical parts of the pegboard, and a few members of a family may have pegboards with overlapping features. However, closer analysis will always reveal that each pegboard is uniquely different from another.

The Pegs

Now, let's consider the pegs of the pegboard to be analogous with sensory experiences—that is, experiences that are perceived by one or any combination of our five senses. The square peg, for example, must be placed into the square slot on the board in order to arrive at a fit. New incoming information to our nervous system is continuous, and the brain, scanning all sensory experiences, attempts to interpret them; it wants to arrive at a "fit." We desperately want to make sense out of this process. However, knowing that all of us have different worldviews, or pegboards, reveals that no two individuals have exactly the same holes or combination of holes. For these reasons, each individual requires a different combination of pegs to achieve a fit.

It is also possible that the identical piece (block) will be interpreted differently among individuals since the holes for that particular block may be found at a different place on the "pegboard" and result in a different meaning. In other words, the same or identical information may be interpreted differently from one person to the other.

Certainly, not all sensory experiences find a fit. There are those stimuli that cannot find a "hole" and are subsequently disregarded. Since each of us is continuously bombarded and inundated with sensory information, all of us continually attempt to make sense out of this information. This process, the continuous sifting and sorting through a myriad of sensory experiences and interpreting them for meaning, is what we term *scanning for a fit.*

As we are flooded with increasing amounts of sensory data, our pegboards change as we experience an increasing amount of sensory data from the world around us. Little Tom's pegboard will change significantly by the time he is "big Tom." In fact, Tom's pegboard may change little by little on any given day. Tom may even interpret information differently from a particular experience in the evening after he's had a meal and some rest, as opposed to the morning after he gets out of bed.

The continual change of the pegboard does not alter the endless process of sorting through information, experiences, and data. Scanning for a fit is an ongoing process that never stops. We constantly attempt to make sense out of a host of sensory experiences, which is no small feat.

The Effects of Metaphoric Teaching

The task of fitting the right pegs into the appropriate holes and sifting through a host of sensory information to make sense out of it is the purpose of the metaphor. This unconscious ritual makes the fairy tale, parable, or allegory such a tremendous tool for influence or change. As soon as the metaphor is presented, the child initiates a search and scans for a fit. At the conscious or unconscious level, each individual attempts to makes sense of it—the kind of sense that has personal meaning, customizing the story for each benefactor.

Even though the process itself is identical for each person, what each individual eventually learns from the story will be different. The child interprets the story in a way that is most fitting with his particular worldview at the time.

The familiar story of *Goldilocks and the Three Bears* may well serve as an example. After hearing the story, Susan, an eight-year-old, may derive that it is not polite to get into other people's business. John, a seven-year-old, may interpret the story to mean that after having gotten into some trouble, one can always "escape" into the comfortable and secure surroundings of one's own home. Five-year-old Mary may simply conclude that one shouldn't go into others' homes. Six-year-old Tom's scanning for a fit may lead him to conclude that adults will always get mad at you. Sever-year-old Heidi, on the other hand, may simply determine that you should not settle for the first thing that comes along but test and try until the right fit has been found.

The specific meaning a child ascribes to a particular metaphor is contingent upon that child's individual world model. But even more important is the fact that the derived meaning contributes to the child's interpretation of the world and provides direction for how one should conduct himself or herself in that world.

In pragmatic terms, the child sifts through the metaphor, looking for meaning, and finds his own meaning through contemplating what the story might imply on a personal level. Depending upon the child's physical and emotional circumstances, such as age, time of day, season, mood, and feelings, the ultimate meaning derived from a particular metaphor may vary.

In the examples above, Mary may have been confronted by her brother about getting into his toys, and hence, her particular way of interpreting the story reflects the idea that one should not intrude into others' homes. John, the seven-year-old, might have gotten into some trouble in the recent past and found that his mother rescued him. To him, the story of the three bears may have further solidified his experience that one can find refuge in familiar places. These diversified applications of the same story teach us that different circumstances create different interpretations.

As part of the maturation process, each child faces different problems or conflicts that youngsters intuitively attempt to solve. When a child is faced with a problem or difficulty—or is currently *stuck*—the child looks about for a solution. The youngster scans both the internal and external world for properties that may aid in the quest for a resolution. The attempt to get *unstuck* is instinctual.

What would happen if a child were presented with a metaphor that somehow resembles the general circumstances of the "stuck" child? Will that child scan the metaphor for a fit? Will she interpret the story, looking for an application of a problem resolution? Will she, when presented with a metaphor, "carve out" certain properties that may provide her with some pointers to solve the problem? The answer is *yes*. In fact, the child will customize the story and bring the solution of the metaphor into alignment with internal conflicts or impasses. The child will superimpose the metaphor to the specific difficulties she is facing.

The youngster will view the "old" problem through the new lens of the metaphor. But, as with every set of glasses, there are those that provide for clearer vision, while others make things even more blurred. The *right* metaphor at the *right* time, and for the *right* problem, may provide the child with a particular new and clearer vision she has been looking for.

A Fresh Approach
to an Old Problem

Depending on the impasse or problem, a particular well-fitting metaphor can be extremely beneficial to a child. Any parent or caregiver wishing to point a youngster in a particular problem-solving direction should not just select any metaphor. Such a parent would, indeed, select one that promises a high likelihood for a proper fit, whereby the child will arrive at a desired meaning.

You may ask whether the content of the metaphor really matters that greatly since the child concludes his own meaning. Remember, however, the meaning is not determined independently of the metaphor. The metaphor provides the fundamental parameter. A closer look at our story will shed some light on this question.

You may have noticed that all the interpretations of the story examples have a central theme, namely that of inappropriate intrusions. While one or the other children may interpret the story along a different theme, it is safe to assume that most interpretations fall in the "intrusion" category.

Hence, the application of a particular, tailored metaphor to a specific problem typically has a greater impact on the child than any story pulled from midair. Each fairy tale or metaphor poses a story problem. Along with the problem, however, a resolution is given. It is precisely the framework of the presenting problem, along with the general direction of the resolution embedded in the metaphor, that guides the listener to the desired outcome. As a result, a custom story, specifically created for a particular child with a particular problem, can be very powerful in assisting that youngster toward finding a solution.

Why "beat around the bush" through relating a metaphor? Why not tell the child explicitly what we want him or her to understand, learn, or simply do? One moves closer to answering this question if one understands that *implicit* directions often produce far less resistance from the child. The metaphor represents a "back door" approach by avoiding the proverbial feedback of "Don't tell me what to do!"

Reducing a Child's Resistance to "Being Told" What to Do

All humans, young and old, have one thing in common: we don't like to be told what to do. The genius of the metaphor, however, provides the youngster to consciously or unconsciously tell himself what to do.

Ordinarily, the undertaking of telling a person what to do may often be met with resistance. The following example may shed some light on the issue. Let us assume that a friend or relative presented you with this book and demanded that you read it. The friend strongly suggested that you should pay close attention as you make your way through the pages, and most importantly, apply the content to your children.

Your reaction is very likely to be one of resistance and may manifest itself in your blatant refusal to read the book. On the other hand, if a friend presented you with the book and suggested you read it because they found it interesting, the probability for your resistance of reading it is significantly lessened. Possibly, the smallest amount of resistance may be encountered if you saw the book in a bookstore, examined it, and decided on your own to read it—as it was your choice. Nobody told you what to do.

In the case of the fairy tale or the metaphor, the idea of "telling the child what to do" is not immediately evident. It is an indirect way of making a suggestion. By the same token, it is important to recognize that we can never get completely away from telling a person what to do, especially when children are involved. Clearly, messages like, *Do this, do that; You ought to consider...; Why don't you...*; or perhaps, *Have you thought of doing it this way?* all communicate a command in the mind of the child.

Some commands may not be immediately recognized as such. For example, consider that in the Jones's house, Mother is setting the dinner table. Without even saying the words, "Come to the table," the simple fact that Mother is setting the table is an implicit message to do so.

The contextual parameters in which a verbal or nonverbal message is sent demand a response. Whenever we demand a response from a person, we, in essence, are telling them what to do. The message of what to do is communicated on either a verbal or a nonverbal level. Since it is impossible for anyone not to communicate, at least nonverbally, commands are inherent in all messages. Telling anyone "what to do" is, therefore, unavoidable.

The person on the receiving end of the message is faced with the decision to either accept the implied command or reject it. If the message is explicit in nature, like "you will" or "I think you should," the likelihood that the child will resist the command is elevated. This is particularly the case with children who are prone to resist being told what to do. Such children often fail to focus on the message but zero in on resistance, which often escalates into an argument and misses the intended message entirely.

The following example will demonstrate this dilemma:

Father: "Son, why don't you ever take the garbage out when your mother tells you to?"

Son: "I don't know. Why you always have to pick on me? What about Mike or Sue? Why don't you pick on them?"

Father: "You always get defensive. I don't like the way you talk to me. This smarting off doesn't cut it with me."

Son: (walks away)

In our example, the father communicated rather explicitly. The command aspect of, "Take the garbage out!" was rather easily recognizable. The son, distracted by the implied parental anger, resists this explicit message. Rather than responding to the issues of taking the garbage out, the son focuses on changing the subject by suggesting an ongoing conflict with his father. The child has been successful in diverting his responsibility of taking out the garbage. What the parent hoped for did not come about. A child who is prone to resist explicit parental direction will find all kinds of distracting behaviors in order to avoid the real issue.

Avoidance of the central issue takes place not only at the conscious level but also at the subconscious level. Some children affirm verbally that they agree with the "command" but subconsciously resent it. Such resistance may come in many forms, such as not finishing the job, poor follow-through, and forgetting or postponing the execution of the command. This does not imply that all children will resist or ignore explicit messages. However, if presented with two messages—one being implicit, the other explicit—the probability for the child to resist the command aspect of the explicit message is simply higher. Conversely, if the command of an implicit message is "hidden" within the message, the probability for compliance improves.

In the metaphor of the fairy tale, the message is hidden. In fact, there really is no specific message until the interpreter of the fairy tale—the child assigns a certain meaning to it. Since, the child discovers the meaning, the chances for resistance are significantly reduced.

In the story of *Goldilocks and the Three Bears*, the commands of *you must, you should,* or *you ought* are buried in the story. Only through the process of scanning for fit does the child assign a meaning, followed by a course of action. The child imposes his own command on himself. If there is to be any dispute regarding that meaning or command, such arguing takes place within the child, rather than between parent and child. Moreover, the camouflaged message of the metaphor encourages the child to pursue a particular course of action, without explicitly telling him so.

The benefits of the implicit commands, inherent in the metaphor, are enormous. Metaphor gets around resistance. It cuts through the layers of opposition. It gets to the heart of the matter without lengthy explanations and verbiage. The "I'll do it my way" approach has always had more disciples than the "You'll do it my way" approach. Children who invest in their own plans for resolution stand to reap more benefits from doing so. Since children are often tired of being told what to do, the metaphor cuts through resistance and speaks to the inner self. It speaks to that part of the brain that allows a child to view the message holistically and to glean the intended meaning.

CHAPTER 5

the two brains

In the previous chapter, we discussed two seminal features of the metaphor—*scanning for a fit* and *reducing resistance*. In this chapter we will focus on an additional important element of the fairy tale with its embedded metaphor. We will discover how the story engages both the left and the right brain.

The story (or the tale) is an artistic "word-painting" that is decoded by the child. Translating such a painting of words into meaning requires the assistance of the brain's right hemisphere. In order to better understand this process, a closer look into the workings of the two hemispheres may be helpful.

The Left Brain

Several decades of scientific research have concluded that if a person is right handed, the left hemisphere, or the left part of the brain, is dominant. It is the "logical half" of the brain, responsible for making sense of a multitude of sensory information and perceptions. The left hemisphere is primarily responsible for speech and language, including grammar, syntax, and semantics. It is responsible for the continuous analytic coding of information into phonetics and semantic properties. The left hemisphere is responsible for reading, writing, computing, counting, etc. It may be referred to as the *logical* or *verbal* part of the brain.

The Right Brain

In contrast, the brain's right hemisphere may be described as the *artistic* or *holistic* part of the brain. Its functions center on being able to envision the overall picture or holistic view, drawing on bits and pieces, or making sense of complex configurations and structures. This ability permits an individual to identify a famous painting simply by viewing only a small portion of it. A person may recognize an entire tune or song by only hearing a few notes. Contestants of the former television game show *Name That Tune* identified a song or piece of music by only hearing a few notes, which tests a person's right hemispheric abilities.

The right hemisphere not only will reveal an entire song, synthesizing it from fragments into a whole, but will also provide the individual with additional sensory recall of particular situations that are associated with the auditory stimuli. For example, a person may listen to a particular song that triggers a number of sensory memories. Among those may include remembering the precise location where the song was first heard. The song may trigger certain emotions and allow the individual to relive elements of that particular time. Conversely, it may be impossible to ask the person to describe details of the above circumstances without listening to the song (a left hemisphere task). The right hemisphere allows one to construct larger thoughts from fragments, completing images from bits and pieces. It is a function of the transformation of abstractions into meaningful, integrated, holistic viewpoints. Interpreting the "word-painting" of the fairy tale and transforming the embedded metaphor into the concrete here and now is predominantly accomplished by the right brain.

Enlisting the Right Brain's Help to Overcome Impasses

A child experiencing an impasse or dilemma has not yet figured out a solution to the problem. While the parent may have the solution, the limited life experience of the child restricts him from solving the issue. In short, the child's worldview does not permit a solution to the problem.

A parent who wants to assist the child in finding a solution to the dilemma has two fundamental approaches to reach the child:

1. Persuade, pressure, counsel, force, enlighten, or teach the child to expand and change the child's worldview.

2. Persuade the child to find the solution within the contextual environment of the child.

CONSIDER THE FOLLOWING EXAMPLE:

Susan, a first grader, refuses to go to school. She is afraid of getting on the bus by herself and is scared of dealing with a host of unfamiliar peers and adults. Under the second option, the parent is faced with the chore of essentially bringing the school to Susan. This may be an impossible task. A parent utilizing the first option, however, may attempt to help Susan change her mind by getting her to perceive the world differently. Such a parent would attempt to change the way Susan interprets the environment around her. This, of course, is not necessarily an easy task but is certainly more promising than bringing the elementary school home.

But what does this have to do with left and right hemispheric activities? Or, how do worldview, environment, and context relate to fairy tales and metaphors? The answer? We make sense of the world around us through the aid of the right brain. It is the right hemisphere that attempts to integrate an enormous amount of data into a coherent picture and transposes the perception of images of the world around us into a whole.

Since identity is directly linked to one's worldview, the right brain may tell us who we are in relation to the environment. It may also tell us what problems or impasses we experience in relation to the context in which we live.

The Right Brain Doing the Right Thing

Attempting to help a child overcome an impasse or problem by utilizing the left hemisphere, employing logic, analysis, argument, and explanation may seem an inferior method to addressing the right hemisphere more directly, as such a method targets *metaphor*.

But remember that the metaphor is an approach that aims to get the child to *think* differently about the world around him—opening the way for the child to find a way over the current hurdle. In doing so, it is the child who finds the way out of the maze, without the parent demanding that he pursue a particular direction. The child teaches himself. He uses his own GPS to get to the desired location. On the other hand, using the left hemisphere approach of direct explanation, logic, indoctrination, argumentation, and confrontation runs a much higher risk of failure.

Knowing that dreams are frequently a right hemispheric activity, an illustration may provide additional understanding.

John has had quite a day. He got up a little late and found himself behind schedule. He had to hurry, but that was not the end of his troubles. There wasn't any hot water with which to wash his face, and when he attempted to brush his teeth, he discovered that the toothpaste tube was empty. Angrily, he threw the tube on the floor, turned around, and accidentally bumped into the bathroom door. He stubbed his toe, and as a result, he could hardly get into his shoes. Now limping, he missed the school bus. Mother ended up driving him to school, and as he walked into the classroom late, John was embarrassed and afraid the teacher might scold him in front of the other children. Luckily, the teacher sensed it was a rough morning, didn't say anything negative, and welcomed him to the classroom. Relieved, John sat down and started his work. That night John had a dream.

He lived in a small house in the middle of the woods. Unlike the other children of the village, he had to walk through an immense, dark forest to get to the village where a few wizards would teach all of the children how to use their swords, mill flour, cook, and attend to the domestic animals.

As he started on the path that led to the village, he sensed some danger. Unlike other mornings, today the clouds hung low, and the morning fog turned the normally visible road into a labyrinth. John realized that he had forgotten to wear his coat and became quite chilled. An owl from a nearby tree flew toward him and screeched. John was surprised and horrified. He had never experienced the forest in such a foreboding way. Anxiously, he ran from the owl but stumbled over a tree stump and fell down. Immediately, he felt the sharp pain in his leg, and just as soon as he reached for his leg, he felt the fear he had of the master wizard who would be angry with him for being late or not showing up at all. But there wasn't anything he could do. The situation seemed hopeless. John was still within shouting distance from the house and yelled for help.

After a few minutes, his father showed up on his horse and helped him up. Together, they rode to the village where the wizard had already started teaching the children. John limped to his usual spot. The wizard, normally tough and unbending, didn't say anything. At first, John was puzzled, but later he understood that the wizard was proud of him for coming in spite of his pain.

John's dream is a typical example of right hemispheric activity. The dream represents a "mental painting"—a holistic, integrated abstraction that is derived from a host of left hemispheric-centered data. John's dream is a metaphoric representation of a host of factual information. His right hemisphere turned it into a "painting." Unconsciously, John was searching for some kind of resolution to hide "the gone foul" day. He needed to process those experiences and provide some feedback for his experience. His dream, the metaphor, gave meaning to his day. He had reached a conclusion.

REAL LIFE	DREAM
Needs to go to school	Needs to attend the wizard's instructions
Runs into problems on the way to school	Runs into difficulties along the trail in the forest
Stubs his toe on the door	Falls over a tree trunk and hurts his foot
Mother comes to help with car	Father comes to help with horse
Teacher, knowing John had problems, does not get angry	Wizard, sensing John had difficulty, does not get angry

In an attempt to demonstrate the usefulness of metaphors, while addressing the right hemisphere, let us consider a John-like situation in reverse. Let us assume that Linda has experienced a day very much like John did. Linda's parents, somewhat annoyed with the situation, may utilize the fiasco-like morning as a teaching experience. In doing so, they fundamentally have two choices in approaching the situation. First, the parents can explain to Linda the pros and cons for getting up on time, being proactive in securing toothpaste, watching where you step, and so on. All of which may assure her of being on time for school and avoiding the wrath of the teacher. This approach, of course, is one that targets the left hemisphere. It is an attempt to teach Linda through reasoning, explanation, analyzing, and indoctrination. There is an attempt on behalf of her parents to persuade Linda to go about her morning routine in a more planned, orderly way. The probability for Linda's resistance to such an approach is high. Linda may find an easy entrance into arguing her point and defending herself against her parents' attempts to tell her what to do. She may, in fact, respond with rationalization, anger, or other means of resistance—all of which may greatly hamper the translation process from the left to the right hemisphere, where the entire incident is integrated into a whole.

Secondly, Linda's parents have the option of attempting to access her right hemisphere by telling her a metaphoric story. The language of the metaphor does not explain, analyze, dictate, or argue. Linda doesn't have to translate left hemispheric information into right hemispheric data. Hence, the probability of her resisting change is significantly reduced. Linda is permitted to deal directly with the essence of her behavior (and connected problems), rather than getting hung up in confrontation with her parents.

The Ever-Present Question: "Why?"

Another not-so-obvious but important aspect of the metaphor is that it does not ask the question *why*. In contrast to asking this question, the metaphor shows the listener what happened and possibly how to go about solving a problem. Metaphors do not focus on *why* but rather on *what,* and they do not mercilessly pursue and press for answers.

A parent who is frequently unsatisfied with a child's inability to answer the *why* question may become impatient and press the child for an answer. If such an answer is not forthcoming, the parent may become angry. As a result, the problem resolution—the strategy of how to go about solving a problem—is forfeited to discussing the infamous question. This can become a pretty complex and frustrating undertaking, leaving both parent and child defeated. To illustrate this point, the following example may be helpful:

Child: Opens the refrigerator door and takes out the milk. In the process, the cup falls to the floor and the milk spills.

Parent: (a little testy) "Tell me, why did you do that?"

Child: (stares at the floor, embarrassed)

Parent: "I wish you would tell me why you did this."

Child: "I don't know" (begins to cry).

Parent: "Why do you keep doing these dumb things? Haven't I told you a thousand times to be careful with the milk?"

Child: "I guess."

Parent: "What do you mean, 'I guess'?"

The answer to the question, "Why did you drop the milk?" is difficult to answer. The confronted child, by now embarrassed, does not want to lose face by surrendering with the obvious answer, "I wasn't careful enough." This, of course, infuriates the parent who demands an answer. Often, the answer must be indicative of some deeper psychological reason behind the behavior. This, of course, the child cannot process. Besides that, answers to the questions of *why* are not resolutions for change. Just because I know why doesn't mean I have changed or that I can change. Many children, and adults, know why they experienced an impasse or a problem, but doing something about it is an entirely different matter.

All the traps of the *why* question can easily be avoided through the metaphor that seldom, if ever, asks that question. More importantly, the metaphor provides the listener with a resolution, a plan of action, a way forward. Metaphors engender hope, and all solutions must first jump over the hurdle called hope.

Ironically, in an attempt to receive an answer to the unanswerable question of *why*, the parent scolds the child for not answering, rather than dealing with the real issue of spilling the milk. Parents who demand answers to *why* questions are only one step up from directly scolding the child for his mishaps or misbehaviors but are still very far away from helping the child overcome, correct, or change a particular behavior. Once again, an example will demonstrate:

Child: (to sibling) "You are so dumb!"

Parent: "Why did you say that to your brother?"

Child: "I don't know … because he's dumb."

Parent: "That's no answer; you better tell me why you said that."

Child: "Leave me alone; ask him."

The question of *why* clearly does not render the type of response the parent expects. In reality, the question sends the child on the defense, and soon the parent and child may argue over who is most defensive, rather than discussing the child's inappropriate comment about his brother. On the other hand, the metaphor—by not asking the question *why*—deals with the real issue. First, this approach addresses the issue of inappropriateness, and secondly, it addresses the issue of corrective action—all embedded within the metaphor. It is not the parent who gives the answer, plan of correction, or advises for better ways of handling the problem. The child, herself, accomplishes the task. The child tells herself what to do.

It can be argued that the child, after having misbehaved, might see the metaphor as having something to do with inappropriate behavior and, hence, may defend against it. In this event, the power of the metaphor is once more demonstrated.

Child: (misbehaves)

Parent: (delivers an appropriate metaphor)

Child: "I know what you are trying to do. You are somehow telling me what to do" (child attempts to put parent in a position of arguing with him).

Parent: "No, I just told you a story."

Child: "Oh no, you're trying to tell me what to do."

Parent: "Well, you have your right to see it any way you wish, but all I have done is told you a story."

By sticking to the metaphor, avoiding the interpretation of the metaphor, and avoiding the *why* question, the parent successfully avoids a confrontation or conflict with the child. More importantly, the probability of the child doing something about the inappropriate behavior has significantly increased by interpreting the metaphor.

Metaphors are indeed powerful. They cause us to think. They gently persuade, influence, and teach. They assist us in changing direction, in regrouping, and in finding solutions to problems. Sometimes, metaphors help us identify solutions for problems to which we've previously been oblivious. It is done through the process of scanning for a fit and by allowing the right hemisphere to be accessed directly. The result is a reduction in resistance, which increases the probability of implementing changes. Lastly, but certainly not least, the metaphor does not get bogged down by the infamous question of *why*.

Metaphor is magic. It works.

Key Terms

Left Brain: The left hemisphere of the brain is responsible for reading, writing, computing, counting, etc. It may be referred to as the *logical* or *verbal* part of the brain.

Right Brain: The brain's right hemisphere may be described as the artistic or holistic part of the brain. Its functions center on being able to envision the overall picture of holistic view to make sense of complex configurations and structures.

Tips:

1. Write a list of recent conflicts with your child.

2. Consider whether or not you elicited the reason for the child misbehavior (i.e., asking the question of *why*).

3. If yes, think of alternative ways to interact with the child by not using the word *why*.

CHAPTER 6

building the foundation

In previous chapters, we discovered how metaphors are fabulous teaching tools. Now we are ready to build the house of the custom fairy tale. We start with the building blocks for the foundation. Putting the right pieces together in the right order allows you to create your own fairy tale with a metaphoric message to help your child through an impasse.

Choosing the Setting

Every story has a setting, one that provides a foundation in which characters may act. Settings place stories in logical frames for understanding. The setting can take a listener to a kingdom in a faraway land or may invite the child to go on a sea voyage. Another setting may beckon a youngster to go on a spaceship adventure.

The setting in which the story takes place is not as important as the story line and the embedded metaphor. Whether the story takes place in a "once upon a time" frame or three billion years into the future does not make an ineffective story better. Therefore, parents or storytellers need not break their backs over the debate of placing the story in the past, present, or future for greater impact. However, since it is impossible not to place the story in a setting, such placement ought to have at least an indirect advantage. Let us consider some possibilities.

Helping to Reduce Resistance

The setting can assist in "hiding the obvious." If the setting is too close to reality, the child may immediately see through the intended message and likely respond with increased resistance. We want the child to ponder and think. This allows the youngster to discover the message on his own. A parent struggling with a child who is intrusive and demonstrates a lack of personal boundaries may choose a *Goldilocks and the Three Bears* approach. On the other hand, if the parent selects a story that highlights a little boy who is interested in many things but messes up other people's things in the process, the setting may be too transparent. This net result creates increased resistance. Much more appropriately, Goldilocks and her mishaps with the three bears takes the problem out of the here and now and places it in an alternate time and space, gives it a new look, changes the characters, adds some talking bears, and achieves the desired effect of making the message less obvious.

Holding the Child's Interest

If the setting of the tale is dull, the net result will be little or no attention on behalf of the child. If the story line is lost, so is the embedded metaphor. What we want to avoid is boredom and the chance for the message to fall on deaf ears. Parents do well when they choose high-interest settings for the child. Michael, who is enthralled with spaceships and computers, may pay closer attention to a story of space warriors, strange creatures, and talking computer chips. Eight-year-old Susan, who borrows her mother's clothes to play kings and queens, may be captured by stories where the content includes princes, kings, commoners, and other kingdom-related props. With an older child who has entered puberty, the story line matters less, as long as it is not obvious to the actual situation.

The Age of the Child

As eluded above, the age of the child is an important factor in choosing the setting. The dynamic interplay between the setting, the embedded metaphoric message, and the age of the child is worthy of further exploration. Once again, Goldilocks will assist in this illustration.

The story will have a very different effect when told to a five-year-old as opposed to a teenager. The reason is simple. A fourteen-year-old is no longer "captured" by three talking bears. On the other hand, the five-year-old may be riveted by the content. To him, the meaning is "hidden" and discovered during the process of "scanning for a fit." Conversely, metaphoric meaning of this story is too transparent for the teenager.

This fact underscores the relationship between the context or setting and the embedded meaning of the metaphor. The more complex the content of the story is, the less transparent the hidden message will be. Conversely, the more the story captures the imagination of the child, the more transparent the embedded metaphor can be.

Remember, there is nothing more powerful than imagination. Historically, nothing has been as powerful to stir the imagination of a listener as a story told in the "classic" form.

The Classic Form

Upon closer examination of fairy tales and stories, we discover that most of them share basic elements. We call these the "classic story form." The classic form invariably consists of a protagonist, who has become the story's hero or heroine after successfully conquering a problem or adversity. Through good fortune, trickery, magic, or great effort, the character strikes success and a hero is born.

The exceptionally beautiful French tale of *Beauty and the Beast* serves as an example.

Long, long ago, in a far-off country, there lived a good merchant who was enormously rich. His wealth had been acquired through years of hard work. Although his wife had died many years before, he felt greatly blessed. His wealth was not what he counted most among his treasure, but his three daughters and three sons, whom he loved deeply. His daughters were attractive, his sons strong and robust. But of all his children, the youngest daughter was by far the most striking, and all who met her called her "Beauty."

The elder daughters were extremely jealous of Beauty. They longed for the attention she received and made every effort to seek attention for themselves. The sisters put on ridiculous airs, dressed themselves in expensive clothes, strutted before mirrors, and complimented themselves on their appearance. But not only was Beauty lovelier than her sisters in appearance, she also had a much kinder and stronger character. She paid little attention to their petty comments. Naturally, this only made her sisters meaner and angrier.

The family's great fortune attracted many eminent men who came to court the girls. The elder daughters, who spurned such attentions, said they would not accept a station less than a duchess or a countess. Beauty was kind to the suitors but told them she was too young to marry and wished to remain with her father for at least a few more years. Besides, she knew she did not feel love for them.

Suddenly, without warning, disaster struck the family. One day they discovered their house in flames. Everything burned to the ground. That same day, the merchant received reports that his vessels at sea were either lost to pirates or in a violent storm. And so, in just one week, the family had fallen from great wealth to dire poverty.

One day, the father got word that one of his ships was thought to be found and so mounted his horse to make the trip to the city, where he hoped to find the ship. Upon his departure, the older sisters demanded their father return with gifts for them, but Beauty only wanted a rose. When the father found the ship, the spices aboard had been completely ruined in the storm; most of the silks and other valuables had been damaged, as well. As the merchant searched through the cargo, his hopes for regaining his wealth dissolved, and he worried bitterly about how he would face his family.

After many weeks of arguments and negotiations, the merchant was left with no money more than what he had carried with him into the city, for what was salvageable from the ship had been claimed by creditors.

Although the trip to the city had been difficult, the way back was even worse. The weather changed from the mild pleasantness of summer to the unpredictable chills of autumn. As the merchant entered a gloomy part of the forest, a bitter storm arose. Howling winds lashed at the trees, and the night grew blacker and blacker until he could barely see the horse's mane before him. Then, suddenly, a light appeared in the distance. As he guided his horse toward the light, a path appeared and at the end stood a magnificent castle bathed in lights. As he climbed the steps to the entrance and entered the great hallway, he came to a startled halt. Before him stood a table set for one, and it appeared to him that he was expected. The guest hoped he might soon be able to thank his benefactor, but no one was to be found, so the merchant fell asleep. The next morning, as he descended the long flight of steps to the courtyard, he noticed an arbor of roses, lovelier and more fragrant than any he had ever beheld. He leaned over a hedge and picked up a large red blossom. "At least," he said, "I will be able to bring this beautiful rose to Beauty." Immedi-

ately a hideous roar resounded in the merchant's ear. Trembling, he turned to see a monstrous creature rushing at him.

"Who said you might take a rose?" the creature gnarled angrily.

White with fear, the merchant responded, "Please, generous lord, I meant no offense. Forgive me. It was only for my daughter. I am only an old man who wishes to please his child, who he has disappointed and failed many times before."

"And your daughter," the creature asked, "she believes you have failed her?"

"No, no," sighed the merchant. "My Beauty is lovelier and finer than your finest rose. She would never complain. Her heart has no room for thoughts of her father's failings, but I have failed her, and I only wish to return to her."

The beast said, "Go to her! If she will agree to come to me and suffer in your place, you shall be free. If not, you must return. Do not try to hide from me, either, for that is impossible," he said. "Go now, go to her. One of you must return to me in two days. If you do not come, I will come for you."

And so the father returned home and told the story to his family.

"No, Father!" his sons exclaimed. "We will return to the beast instead and destroy this ugly monster."

"No, my sons, the power of the beast is too great. There is no chance you could accomplish such a feat."

Beauty replied, "I must go, and I will."

As Beauty and her father prepared to leave the next morning, her brothers again protested, but they couldn't hold Beauty back. Finally, after a long day's ride, the travelers arrived at the castle. They heard the groaning sound of the large door opening. The beast's low steps echoed down the hallway. The merchant watched his daughter's face freeze in apprehension and lamented his inability to protect her. Beauty stared, transfixed at the entrance to the room, and her eyes widened in horror as the creature entered. Despite all the efforts she had made to prepare herself, the beast was, indeed, far worse than she had imagined.

"I am pleased," said the beast. "As for you, old man," he continued, turning to the merchant, "you shall stay only this night. Rise quickly in the morning and take your breakfast. When the bell rings, you must depart."

And so the next morning, the father went home. The next day, Beauty did not see any evidence of the beast. And as she descended her room for dinner, she was surprised to find a place set for only one. She ate her dinner, which she found most delicious, and it was only when she had finished that she heard the noise of the beast.

"Might I stay and talk with you?" he asked.

"Well yes, of course, if that is what you wish," said Beauty.

"It is not what I wish but what you wish. This is your castle now. You are to be the mistress here. You need but bid me leave, and I will obey immediately. Do you think me terribly ugly?"

The beast's stare was so intense that Beauty felt herself flush with confusion and could barely reply.

"Yes, that is true."

The beast's sigh was long and heavy. "I know. It is true. Besides, how foolish my hopes and desires are. I'm a stupid, horrible creature."

Beauty glanced at the beast. His huge, hairy chest rose and fell in deep sighs. Mixed with fear, she felt compassion for her captor for the first time. Later that evening, the beast approached Beauty. His next words sent a chill through her. "Beauty, will you be my wife?"

It was some time before she dared answered him. She sat with her face turned away, struggling to master her feelings of shock and repulsion. She reared, angering him. At last, she managed to say softly, "No, I cannot."

"Farewell then, Beauty," said the beast, and he left the room with heavy dread and many longing glances at her. The beast told her she could have the castle and all that was in it. She decided to stay. Still, she could not keep from dreading the beast's arrival every evening after dinner. She feared that his bestiality at any moment might break the restraint under which he kept himself. After a few days, however, she came to know that, although he asked each evening the awful question, "Beauty, will you be my wife?" with passion trembling behind his voice, he always accepted her refusal without anger.

The sadness and his quiet resignation to the pain of this rejection touched Beauty's gentle heart and greatly lessened her repugnance for him. With each visit, his singular appearance seemed less fearsome. More and more, she felt his rough voice and movements did not altogether reflect his heart and spirit.

One day, Beauty took a walk in the enchanted forest by the castle and, finally tired, fell asleep. When she awoke, she found herself in her own bed at her father's house. Her father was nearly overcome with shock at the sight of his dear daughter. She threw her arms around him, crying and laughing in happiness. "Father," she cried, "my dear father."

"Come, Beauty, sit down, and tell me what happened. Are you all right? Were you safe from the horrible creature?"

"Yes. Yes, Father, I am fine," she said. "And the beast is not a horrible creature. He is actually kind and gentle. I must go back." Beauty visited with her family, but after a few days, the time for Beauty's departure drew near.

Her father spoke again of the beast. "Beauty," he asked, "are you sure you wish to return to the beast? It must be very frightening for you."

"At first it was. Indeed, I would tremble every time he came into the room. But Father, he is so gentle. He would never harm me. And after a while, I found I really enjoyed talking to him. Sometimes he is funny and makes me laugh. Other times, though, he seems really sad, and I must turn away from him so as not to cry myself. I only wish he would not always ask me to marry him."

The next night, Beauty had a frightening dream. She found herself in the castle's garden. From behind some bushes, she heard painful groans. "What's that?" she cried, carefully running down a stone path. There, behind the bushes, was the beast in agony. He looked at her, reproachfully asking, "Beauty, why have you treated me so? Why have you broken your word? Why have you broken my heart?" And then he spoke no more.

Beauty awoke from her sleep and burst into tears. "What have I done to my dear beast? How could I have waited so long to return to him? He is so kind and good, and though he is ugly, how could he be blamed? Have I been so blind? Have I killed him? How wicked I am. I cannot stand it."

Beauty returned to the castle, but the beast was nowhere to be found. Beauty ran from the castle out into the grounds. Past the rose bushes, up and down the path, she flew, calling for him in vain. The silence of the castle that she had grown so accustomed to seemed to mock her now. Exhausted, she sank to the ground and began to sob. Then, suddenly, she saw him lying still and quiet on the ground, seemingly dead.

In despair, Beauty fell to the ground beside him, weeping bitterly. She stroked his hairy face, and the tears from her eyes fell to his cheeks. Slowly, the beast's eyes opened. His voice was faint and faltering. "Beauty, have you come back to me?"

Her heart pounded. "Beast, please do not die. I love you. Live for my sake. From this moment I vow to be your wife. I could not bear to be without you."

No sooner were these words spoken than fireworks exploded in the sky and the sound of beautiful music filled the air. Beauty looked up, dazed. Her eyes darted from the castle to the sky, and her mind raced in confusion. Turning to the beast, she drew back in shock from the sight that greeted her. The beast was gone, and before her stood the handsome prince of her dreams. "Where is my beast?" she gasped.

"Before you, Beauty," said the prince. "I was the beast. Many years ago a wicked fairy condemned me to remain in that form until a beautiful woman would consent to marry me. I could not reveal my plights to her. Of all souls, only you were generous enough to see me as I am. You are selfless enough to devote your life to me. Your understanding and virtue and love are beyond compare. Beauty, I love you deeply and all I have I give to you."

Beauty sent for her family to come to the castle. And the prince married Beauty, and they lived happily ever after.

To show love for something as utterly ugly as a beast, at first, was simply unthinkable for Beauty. But over time, with persistence, the young woman discovered that true love is not contingent on appearance but on compassion. She discovered that love is measured not by the external condition but by internal properties. Through the story and its embedded metaphor, Beauty reaps the unanticipated rewards by having overcome her fears. This is an example of the "classic" form of a tale.

Key Term

Classic Form: A story of a protagonist, who through good fortune, trickery, magic, or great effort overcomes adversity to become the story's hero.

Tips:

Reflect on a recent or ongoing conflict with your child, and look for a story, or stories, in classic form that relates to the conflict. Try to write down at least one embedded metaphor from the story that may help your child become the hero of his or her own story.

CHAPTER 7

adding to the infrastructure

In earlier chapters, we established the core elements of a story and discussed context and the classic form. By adding additional elements, we widen the applications for "helping" metaphors through tales, stories, and other means. In this chapter, we will discuss how a story's language, characters, events, and format contribute to its metaphorical messages reaching a young audience.

Flowery Language

Keeping a child's attention through the selection of a stimulating context is important. Carefully chosen language increases a child's focus, and we want the child completely immersed in the story. To accomplish this task, a child must become involved through imagination, and imagination is enhanced with *flowery language*.

One could likely convey the essential facts and message of the story of *Beauty and the Beast* on a single sheet of paper. So why the flowery language, the excessive verbiage? Because the language provides imagery, which deepens the imagination of the listener and draws the child further into the story. In short, descriptive language stimulates the imagination of the child.

In part, both the magical power of the fairy tale and the delight we experience while listening come from the literary qualities—the flowery language. It is in the way a story is told that often evokes interest and involvement. By not rushing from key points to conclusion, a sense of anticipation is created that helps make the child a better listener and participant. This process increases attention to the central message of the metaphoric meaning.

The tale, aside from its meaning, often resembles a work of art. In fact, some child psychiatrists suggest that the true meaning and impact of a fairy tale can only be fully experienced by the child when the story is in its "complete" form—indicating that the tale and the embedded metaphor are most effective if the tale is related in an unabridged manner. In other words, we want the full story, not the short version. Just conveying raw, skeletal data essential to the central understanding of the metaphor provides the listener with little emotional involvement. Remember, the deeper the involvement or imagination, the better the child will retain the story, along with the embedded message.

We want the child not only to hear the words of the story but to *experience* the tale as well. Flowery language invites the child to experience an event by involving as many senses as possible. Moreover, the more diverse sensory details the child experiences as the story is told, the greater the chances for the story to impact the child.

The long, flowery story of *Beauty and the Beast* is an attempt to create impact. This form conjures up an aura and sets a tone, or mood, essential for the complete understanding of the metaphor. Sensory details create imagery for listeners that, in turn, propels imagination.

It is for this reason that the storyteller, choosing the classic form, should employ language that is imaginative, flowery, and very generous with incidental and idiosyncratic information. Clothing the bare bones of the metaphor in a poetic, attractive, attention-getting language enriches the story and understanding.

On the other hand, not all metaphors (in an effort to reach their optimal effectiveness) need to appear in the classic form. In fact, there are endless stories and tales that have metaphoric properties without employing the "hero conquers a problem" theme. Such messages are referred to as "statement form" metaphors.

The Statement Form

Not all stories, tales, parables, or fables that contain metaphoric messages follow the classic form. There are metaphors that simply make a statement, communicate an idea or a truth, or provide an element of wisdom. The story of *Goldilocks and the Three Bears* is indicative of such a statement form. Our little blonde "monster" encounters a situation by entering a house. She behaves inappropriately by intruding on another's property, and when danger appears in the form of three bears, she escapes the situation and runs to the security of her own home. Thus, the story does not follow the classic form. Goldilocks does not resolve an obstacle and reap unexpected rewards, indicative of the classic form metaphor. In this case, the statement form simply seeks to communicate an idea. The statement form conveys a statement. Such a statement could be: *don't be intrusive; show respect for another's property; don't wander far away from home or you will get into trouble; or sometimes you get into trouble, but you can always come home again.*

Another example may further clarify this point. Some years ago, I sat at a club luncheon eagerly waiting the guest speaker to finish his speech. The anticipatory anxiety about all the unfinished work awaiting me at my desk interfered with my ability to listen to the lecturer's message. I have long since forgotten the general content of the speech, but to this day, I can remember the punch line of the poem the speaker recited at the end of his speech. The statement that "it's better to have a fence on top of the mountain than an ambulance in the valley below" has firmly embedded itself in my long-term memory.

This phrase illustrates the statement form metaphor. The sentence does not pose a problem awaiting a hero to solve, nor does it speak of riches and happiness at the end of a difficult journey. Such a metaphor simply makes a statement—one that is contingent on the person's "search for a fit" and can be interpreted in many different ways. The result of such a search may render the interpreter to conclude that *appropriate prevention may significantly reduce the probability of injury.* Another reaction may be that *it is cheaper to pay for preventive measures than for the costs associated with damages.* Yet another listener may insist that *if you prepare for the worst, the worst has less of a chance to happen.*

Searching for a fit and finding the embedded meaning in an idea is not restricted to the classic form of metaphor. Poems, sayings, or simple metaphoric ideas have inevitably the same effect. Regardless of the apparent differences between classic and statement forms, the powerful impact of the metaphor—in its search for a fit is evident. Each embedded metaphor finds a custom fit with every child in need of solving a riddle. To facilitate this process, one needs to carefully consider matching characters and events. This aids the child, or listener, in "fitting" himself into the story or situation.

Matching Characters and Events

The listener of a tale, consciously or unconsciously, sees himself woven into the fabric of the story. This is the case for the classic and the statement forms of the metaphor. In short, the child identifies with a character in the story or applies the situation of the statement form himself. Of course, when creating a custom story, the storyteller must "guide" the child to identify with the "right" character. Such an identification process is related to the relative closeness of the child's own life situation compared to that of the story.

The child sees his own reflection in the waters of the tale, and contingent upon the particulars of the story, identifies other significant characters or associated elements. In short, the significant others in the child's life are found among the cast of the tale. The same process is true for the setting and sequence of events, both within and outside of the metaphor.

It is important, however, to understand that too close a match between real life and the metaphoric situation destroys the very purpose of the metaphor. If characters and situations in the story are too closely related to the real life setting of the child, the "searching for a fit" process has been compromised. The net effect is that the child will easily see through the metaphor and uncover the "lecture," thereby increasing the probability of becoming defensive in a number of different ways. Nevertheless, a story with inherent characters and settings should somehow resemble those of a child's life setting.

A resemblance, rather than a close fit between real life and story, will "hide" the direct message and allow the child to contemplate the lesson free of perceived parental interferences. Metaphoric representations of real-life characters are endless. Here are just a few:

LIFE CHARACTER	METAPHORIC CHARACTER
Child	fawn, cadet, or prince/princess
Mother	doe, lieutenant, or queen
Father	buck, captain, or king

Of course, the identification of the above characters alone is not sufficient to build the kind of tale we want to tell our children. We want to build tales and stories with embedded metaphors that are tools for change. Only through the dynamic interplay of the characters in the tale can the child capture the metaphoric message that is key to change. In telling a story—or more specifically, in building an effective metaphor for change—the parent must be aware of characters and how those characters interact and behave.

Let us consider the following example:

Susan is at an age where she will attend kindergarten. Yet, she appears somewhat frightened about the prospect of leaving home and embarking

on the "big wide world." Her parents, knowing Susan very well, under-
stand she has a strong desire to learn and explore. They know that Susan
is a "pleaser" and that she will be disappointed if she is unable to please
her teacher with regular, active school attendance. In short, Susan has
misgivings about going to school. She is also "headstrong" and insists in
doing things by herself without help from others. She appears stuck.

The direct teaching method for helping Susan overcome her "stage fright" likely lies within the parameters of encouragement. The traditional approach relies on parental support of Susan, telling her that she has nothing to be afraid of. The approach will include the rationale that she likes to learn, is eager to approach new tasks, and pleases people and herself in the process. Her parents may try to convince her that she will be okay, that her teacher will not bite, and that other children have come out of the same situation unscathed.

In most cases, this form of encouragement may take care of the problem. But let us consider that in a vicious cycle, Susan's anxieties about school increase proportionately with each wave of new encouragement. In Susan's mind, this increased parental encouragement may signal that there is really something to be afraid of.

Under such circumstances, the story—with its embedded metaphoric message—may render better results. Here, then, are some building blocks for the creation of a metaphoric fairy tale designed to assist Susan in helping her find answers to her dilemma.

LIFE SITUATION	METAPHORIC REPRESENTATION A	METAPHORIC REPRESENTATION B
Father	Papa Eagle	King
Mother	Mama Eagle	Queen
Susan	Eagle Chick	Princess
Susan demonstrates anxiety about school attendance	Eagle chick is frightened to learn how to fly	Princess does not want to leave castle
Parents encourage her to go to school	Papa and Mama eagle teach the chick to fly	In a carriage, the king and queen take the princess on a tour and show her the entire kingdom
Susan shows more anxiety	The chick is scared and does not want to learn to fly	The princess hides under the seat of the carriage

The examples show the transformation of the real-life situation into various metaphoric settings of an eagle family and a kingdom with supporting characters. Whether a parent chooses the eagle family or the kingdom setting is less significant than how the characters ultimately relate and interact with each other, which will be discussed later. The metaphoric message containing the "escape of the dilemma" lies in the interaction of the three primary characters. Matching real-life circumstances to story characters is paramount. At the same time, the context or setting of the story facilitates the involvement of the child in the story play. Indeed, the context or setting of the story can take on endless possibilities.

Let us consider another example.

Tom, a five-year-old boy, acts strangely after his mother brings her new baby girl home from the hospital. Tom does not want to have anything to do with the baby. On some occasions, Mother discovers that Tom kicks the crib. When a toy or a cloth animal falls out of the crib, Tom carelessly throws it back in. Tom's strange behaviors predictably escalate whenever his mother is in the process of feeding the baby. Tom always manages to interrupt the feeding process with his antics.

LIFE SETTING	METAPHORIC CHARACTERS AND EVENTS
Mother	Mama rabbit
Tom	Fred, the big brother rabbit
Baby girl	Little-bitty, wee rabbit
Mother brings the baby home from the hospital	One day, after Fred returns home from playing outside, he finds a wee baby rabbit in the nest
Tom acts antagonistic toward the baby	Fred feels bad that Mom and Dad are no longer playing with him alone
Tom throws toys back into the crib	Whenever mother rabbit is gone, Fred pushes the baby rabbit in the far corner of the nest

The metaphoric setting of a rabbit family with a new baby rabbit is applied to a similar real-life situation involving Tom. Once again, the setting is of limited significance in relationship to the dynamic interplay of the characters in the story. While our little jealous friend, Tom, is likely to pay close attention to a story of rabbits, Tom, our five-year-old, likely has limited insight into his response toward the new arrival in the home. He will learn much more from the rabbit story than a "get away from the baby" or "leave the baby alone" response from his parents. Also of significance is the fact that the metaphoric tale of the rabbit family is a positive approach to problem solving. After all, the message of *don't* invites resistance more so than the message of *do*.

Negative and Positive Language

The language a parent chooses to utilize in conveying a message to a youngster can essentially be framed in a positive or negative light. The message of *do* conveys the meaning that one ought to behave in a new or alternative way, while the message of *don't* asks for a discontinuation of "bad" behaviors. Behavioral scientists know that it is easier to entice a person to engage in new, alternative behaviors than to eliminate maladaptive behaviors. For this reason, the storyteller needs to make an effort to clothe the story and embedded metaphor in positive language.

To illustrate, let us assume that a mother is frustrated with her thirteen-year-old daughter, Cathy, who constantly overeats. In an attempt to curb Cathy's habits, Mother has, fundamentally, two approaches that may encourage her daughter.

- "Cathy, you should stop overeating because if you don't, you are going to be overweight. You will be less mobile and you will not be able to run as fast as your friends. They might make fun of you. Furthermore, your health may be in jeopardy, as you may develop all kinds of unhealthy physical symptoms."

- "Cathy, if you eat less, think of how much healthier you will feel. You will be in great physical shape, you will be able to breathe easier, and your friends will think of you as a person who takes care of herself."

The first example is essentially an effort to discourage the child from overeating because of potential negative impacts. The latter guides Cathy toward the positive aspects of a balanced diet. The first option discourages the child, telling her to stop. The latter entices the child to change her eating habits with a positive, proactive approach.

Sometimes it is difficult to frame the story in positive language. Nevertheless, positive language renders better results. Moreover, the chances for resistance are typically greater with a negative-language approach. A "don't" language approach carries with it a certain level of criticism, to which most people respond with apathy. On the other hand, the positive language pattern avoids criticism and negative implications of certain behaviors and encourages the child to change behavior by looking toward the "bright side."

The emphasis on the positive language is typically more prevalent in fairy tales. The stories of Goldilocks and Beauty document this point. In both examples, story lines do not emphasize what the protagonist (central character) should *not* have done. In the case of *Beauty and the Beast*, the emphasis targets positive implications of Beauty's "heroic" behaviors. There is a message of what is positively going to happen if one behaves in a certain fashion, rather than addressing negative outcomes if one continues in unproductive or inappropriate behaviors.

The storyteller may profit by using positive language patterns in an attempt to assist the child through an impasse or obstacle. The clever storyteller knows that she has an easier "sell" if she wraps the message of change in sugarcoated, positive language.

CHAPTER 8

bridging the river

A well-constructed story, with its embedded metaphor, has the power to help a child overcome a problem, point her in the direction of a solution, or give her new hope to conquer an impasse. The key that makes the metaphor therapeutic is the *strategy* employed by the storyteller. It is the bridge from *problem* to *solution*.

The Strategy

The strategy of the metaphor is the way the storyteller builds the bridge from the problem to the resolution. It is the key that opens the door for change. The strategy is a central element that describes *how* or *what* the hero does to reap the unexpected rewards of his behavior.

A marginally effective metaphor simply "confronts" the child with new or desired behaviors, paying little or no attention to *how* or *what* must be done to achieve the changed state.

In a previous example, Susan, who has anxiety, avoids going to school. A non-effective strategy resembles the following example:

LIFE SITUATION	METAPHOR
Susan shows more anxiety about going to school. She begins to trust her parents, feels encouraged, and goes to school.	The eagle chick is afraid to learn how to fly. One day, the young eagle chick begins to fly.

Here, the young eagle suddenly, without apparent reason, begins to fly. Such a spontaneous recovery is not likely to take place. This metaphor does not offer Susan a "bridge" to overcome her fears.

An effective metaphor provides the listener with strategy, a way to go about solving the problem. The bridge from problem to resolution exists in many forms, all having their unique and appropriate places, contingent upon the circumstances of the child. In the example of *Beauty and the Beast*, the key to recovery is Beauty's relentless endurance and compassion that lead to change and ultimate happiness.

Encouragement

Perhaps the simplest form of bridge building is *encouragement*. This strategy may be used most optimally if and when the child is already on the right track but requires a little push along the way. It is offered to the youngster who is already going down the path to problem resolution but gets discouraged during the process because the road may be troublesome, lonely, or frightening. Such a child may simply need a dose of encouragement.

Drawing upon the example of Susan and her school anxiety, let us assume that she has made a variety of attempts to solve the problem. She may have gone to the bus stop a number of times but chickened out at the last minute and returned home. Or she may have gone to school but ended up at the nurse's office, professing a stomachache and demanding to return home again. Susan's parents, who may be frustrated by having to pick her up from school, should be rather encouraged with her progress to overcome her fears.

In this case, a simple metaphor with the bridge communicating the message of, "Keep up the good work and you will eventually succeed," may be all that is necessary to help Susan resolve her residual anxieties about school. A story utilizing the encouragement metaphor may resemble the following example.

One day a very young eagle tried to fly on his own. It was a big day for him. All the other birds came to see him. Everyone knew the big day had arrived. He was scared and frightened inside. For a moment, he thought he wouldn't try, but he knew that, sooner or later, he had to. After all, all the birds had come out to watch him. And so he tried. It wasn't a big flight. As a matter of fact, it was only from one tree to the next, but that was all he had to do as an eagle on his first flight.

All along, the young eagle was very frightened, and he thought to himself: "What will happen if my wings don't carry me that far?"

But somehow the courage deep down inside himself won out. He carefully walked to the end of the branch, and with his eyes firmly fixed on a particular limb of the other tree, he spread his wings and pushed off. His eyes were glued to the branch on the other tree, and all his thoughts were centered on exactly where he would come to rest on the branch. "The branch is so far away," he thought.

Suddenly, he discovered that he was gliding through the wind. "I'm flying, I'm flying!" he yelled. He was so excited that for a moment he forgot to beat his wings and took a plunge. But just before he hit the ground, he spread his wings again and flew like an airplane. He was flying. He was in control. It only took a few beats of his wings for the eagle to glide through the air and rest upon the branch he had chosen before he pushed off.

After the young eagle perched, he felt so much excitement that he did not want to fold his wings. The mother eagle, resting in the nest, signaled to him to fold his wings, but he kept them spread. He wanted to enjoy the moment, this glorious moment of his first flight. Then the little eagle, so proud of his accomplishment, stuck out his big chest, folded his wings down, and said over and over again, "I've done it! I've done it! I've done it!"

In the above example, the bridge of encouragement is not deeply hidden and may be easily recognized by the listener. The reason for this is that the child has already turned the corner toward improvement. The eagle story is a reaffirmation of what is already in progress.

In a case where a child has made little to no improvement toward a desired goal, the simple message of "keep up the good work" will not be enough. If Susan had made no attempts to go to school, the eagle story would be inappropriate. In such a case, she may benefit from the strategy of *reframing*.

Reframing

In an effort to assist in the discussion of reframing, let us again draw upon Susan and her fear of going to school. You will recall that Susan has a fundamental desire to attend school but is frightened. One of the fears appears to be related to disappointing her teacher.

The reality is that Susan *thinks* she is afraid. In all cases, any emotion, including fear, is first triggered by a thought. Susan has never experienced school and, therefore, cannot draw on her experiences. She *thinks* she is afraid. Perhaps Susan has gone so far as to conceptualize that if she can rid herself of this fear, everything will be all right. Whether this is the case or not, eliminating the emotion of fear certainly brings Susan a great deal closer to her goal of school attendance. But rather than attempting to plead with her to give up her fears, which may be a laborious task, convincing Susan that fear is not a deficit but an asset may render better results. If this task can be accomplished, she will no longer have to fear her fear. Susan will be able to go on with business and attend school.

Changing the commonly perceived notion of fear from a negative emotion into something useful, positive, and beneficial is precisely what the strategy of *reframing* is all about. Reframing is the task of changing the meaning of a word. In our case, reframing means to attach the fear to a new meaning. Reframing is to take what the child perceives to be painful, bad, or undesirable and cast it in a new, positive light.

Unintentionally, most parents have used this method with relative frequency in one form or another. It is nothing magical or complicated. An example or two will instantly bring about recognition.

John runs into the kitchen, screaming at the top of his lungs. Between his tears and intense distress, his mother determines he has fallen down and scraped his knee. Following her quick examination, she is satisfied that a trip to the emergency room can be avoided in favor of a little ointment and a Band-Aid. To assist John in overcoming his trauma, Mother may present the following reframes:

"John, I bet that really hurts. Tell me…how did you do this?"

Following his explanation, "My goodness, you could have really hurt your leg. If that would have been the case, you wouldn't be able to walk and I would have had to take you to the hospital. I guess you are really lucky, aren't you?"

"Gee, John, look at that blood, here. This tells me you have really healthy blood. Look what a healthy color that blood has. See how red it is? That is a sign that you're really strong, healthy, and tough."

These responses to John's distress reframe the situation. Notice the key strategy of turning something bad into something good by changing the *meaning* of the experience. Mother accomplishes this task by recognizing that the child is hurt. If she neglects to acknowledge her child's pain, John may cry louder to prove that he is truly hurt. Rather than focusing on the pain, Mother draws the attention to something positive, thereby changing the perception of the experience. The net effect of changing John's perception will result in a change of emotion. Remember, first is the thought, followed by the emotion.

You will notice that Mother never insists John is fine, nor does she push her agenda down his throat. John is left to come to this conclusion all by himself. The clever mother is simply changing the *meaning* of the experience.

Let's look at another example of the reframing strategy.

Mike and Tom are brothers. Mike is ten, and Tom is nine. They fight constantly by punching and shoving each other. These instances have become rather annoying to their parents, who have attempted to stop them from fighting by separating them. This, in turn, has made matters worse. Getting their hands on each other is even more of a challenge than before—and the fighting persists.

The following example may be a possible reframe:

"You know, guys, I have been watching you for quite some time. The longer I watch you, the more I become convinced that you really don't hate each other, but love each other very much. You guys like each other so much that you want to be together continuously. You may be somewhat embarrassed about this great need you have to be together, and that's probably the reason you act like you are fighting. Let's face it, you love each other, and I am glad about that!"

The reframe is easily recognizable as the parent turns fighting (aggression and hate) into a manifestation of love (the need to be together at all costs). As in the previous example, the parent changes the meaning of the behavior with the two brothers. Moreover, the parent "proves" to the boys that they love each other by the fact that they can't keep their hands off each other through fighting. The brothers can only disagree with the "love message" by no longer fighting and harassing each other.

Reframing can be a very powerful strategy in assisting the child with discovering a solution to perceived problems.

Let's draw one more time on the previous example of Susan and her school anxiety. Utilizing the previous eagle story, a possible reframe strategy may be as follows:

It first appeared to everyone that the young eagle's reluctance to fly was simply fear of trying something new. Everyone thought the young eagle behaved more like a chicken than an eagle. But the longer others thought about it, and the longer they talked about it, the more they discovered they were mistaken. What others thought of and interpreted as fear turned out to be something quite different.

Both the mother and father eagle flew away for a short time to talk to an old eagle they knew. The old eagle was a flight instructor and had taught many young eagles to fly. When the eagle parents told the instructor about their young eagle that had trouble learning to fly, they received the most unexpected answer. He told them of a young eagle he once knew. Everyone thought that this young eagle was afraid too, but in reality that eagle was not really afraid at all. That young eagle wanted to do so well that he was overcome with a great deal of desire. "You see," said the old flight instructor, "that eagle didn't want to just be another eagle; he wanted to be a real expert flyer." This eagle was so concerned, and cared so much about how good of a flyer he would become, that he was hesitant to proceed.

Again, the fundamental elements of the reframe are easily recognizable. First, the storyteller recognizes the "hurt." The parent wants to reassure the child that they know what the matter is and are aware of the problem. Before the child considers any alternatives, it is important for him to know that someone cares and understands.

Notice, however, that this recognition process is embedded in the metaphor of learning to fly. Thus, if the child shows any resistance, that resistance is not directed at the parents. After all, the parents are talking about eagles and flying and not school phobia.

Secondly, fear is transformed into care and intense desire. It is the intense care and desire that makes the child proceed with caution and constraint. It is important that the storyteller takes adequate time to explain the connection between negative and positive elements.

Reframes are as countless as the imagination of the storyteller. The key to successful reframing is the ability to make plausible connections between the perceived negative—to the positive. Here is yet another possible reframe, using the same general theme of learning to fly.

The eagle family had two young eagles. They were to be equally mighty and vigorous, ready to take on the big skies. It appeared that nothing stood in their way of becoming a few of the greatest flyers in the valley.

One day, Xavier, the magic owl, came for a visit. He came to all the young birds everywhere and bestowed them with gifts. Some birds were endowed with beautiful feathers, others with exceptional voices. Some were given the gift of speed, and others were given the ability to jump high. And so the time had come for the magic owl to pass out the gifts for the two young eagles. Theodore, the boy eagle, was endowed with an extraordinary wingspan that automatically gave him the potential to become one of the most majestic flyers ever to live in the valley. He had the potential to fly higher and travel longer distances than most other eagles. Theodore excitedly thanked Xavier.

Then Xavier turned to Anna, the girl eagle. Her eyes were wide open with anticipation, anxiously awaiting her gift. "To you, Anna, I'm going to give a very special gift, a gift that I have only given on very rare occasions."

"I'm ready, I'm ready," said Anna. She was so excited she almost burst with joy. Xavier reached out with one of his wings and touched Anna on both eyes. Instantly, Anna was blind.

"You'll see me when you've discovered your gift," said Xavier, and with that he departed.

At first Anna was disappointed and cried, "I didn't get a gift! I got a curse!" For weeks, she sat in the nest crying, feeling unable to do anything. She thought she could never fly. As the weeks went by, however, Anna grew more and more restless. Sitting around and waiting for something to happen had become too boring. Her desire to fly grew stronger and stronger, and one day she stood at the edge of the nest, flapping her wings.

"Push off!" said the mother eagle. "I will talk to you so you can hear my voice and fly back to the nest."

To everyone's surprise, Anna took flight. Of course, on that first flight, she did not fly very high, nor did she fly too far, because she needed to orient herself by the voice of her mother eagle. However, every day Anna flew a little higher and a little farther. The fact that she could not see forced her to pay close attention to how her wings were affected by the wind. She learned to pay attention to each single feather on her wings and how to move them in effort to circle, land, and start. Day by day, she grew into a magnificent flyer.

Meanwhile, Theodore knew his marvelous potential to become a great flyer, but he did not practice nearly as much as Anna did. Many times he preferred to stay at home or play with other eagle children. In fact, his flying habits became sloppier, while Anna's became more magnificent. Every bird in the valley began to notice her, and all were astonished by her incredible abilities.

One day Anna and Theodore left the nest at the same time. They flew high above the valley. Suddenly, they noticed dark clouds rolling up into the skies, and a strange wind came up. In no time, Anna and Theodore were tossed around by the wind. Theodore, not able to control his wings well enough, got turned upside down and fell out of the sky. Anna could hear him crying for help. Amid the winds and the rain, she swooped down and found Theodore with a broken wing, lying in a bush. Anna sat beside her brother until the winds and the rain died down. Then Anna picked up Theodore with her talons, flapped her wings as hard as she could, and flew back toward the nest.

By now, word had gotten around in the valley, and when Anna arrived at the nest with Theodore in tow, all the birds were waiting. They chirped in excitement. One could hear them from miles away. "You are the greatest flyer in the sky," they chimed in unison. "Never have we seen anything like this." All the birds of the valley gathered around the nest, and when the magical wise owl reappeared, a hush fell over the crowd.

Xavier approached Anna. "You have done well," he said. And then with his great wings, he touched her eyes. Anna could see again. For a moment she stood there, without any movement.

"Only now do I know what great gift you have given me," she said as a tear rolled down her beak.

Xavier smiled and disappeared into the forest. A celebration was held for Anna that day—and for years to come the story was told among all the birds in the valley.

The metaphor of Anna represents another reframe, a strategic bridge to get from problem to resolution. In this case, a negatively perceived situation of blindness is turned into strength and accomplishment. As the metaphor implies, only through the handicap is our heroine able to develop the kinds of talent and strength she displays. Weakness is transformed into strength, and a negative situation is reframed to become positive. The continued practice of reframing assists listeners in seeing potential elements within problems that not only provide hope but also propel change.

CHAPTER 9

more ways to cross the river

Chapters 1 through 8 systematically introduced and examined the components of constructing a story with an embedded metaphoric message. In this chapter, and those that follow, we will demonstrate how these components come together in a holistic form to create engaging stories with accessible metaphors that both educate and inspire a young audience. As we have already discussed in previous chapters, the result of such storytelling can have a tremendous impact on a child's motivation and ability to overcome relevant problems and obstacles in his or her own life.

Turning Lemon into Lemonade

A reframe is built on the notion of turning something negative into a positive. One "accepts" the "negative" or "undesirable" from the youth but attaches a different and new meaning to the behavior or thought. Consequently, the child is invited by the story to change the behavior. Here is an example:

Eight-year-old Tommy is observed having difficulty approaching new tasks. His piano teacher reports that every time a new piece of music is presented, Tommy appears aggravated and short tempered. However, once Tommy gets into the piece, these undesirable behaviors disappear. His classroom teacher reports a similar pattern. When a new concept in math or science is introduced, Tommy often becomes disrespectful with the teacher. However, once the class is immersed in the subject matter, Tommy's anger disappears. It is evident to the parents and teachers that Tommy is threatened and feels anxious when tackling new tasks.

Below is a story with an embedded metaphoric message utilizing the reframing strategy. Remember, reframing takes a potentially negative situation and makes it positive. In the example, the story appears in the left column. The right column contains a running commentary and description of the story.

Please note that any of the preceding stories can and should be embellished, following the principle of flowery language as discussed in chapter 7. For the sake of space, the story here is held to fundamentals.

THE STORY	COMMENTARY

On the third moon of the planet Knob, there lived a king and a queen. The planet Knob was in the middle of the galaxy next to the Fishtail nebula, and the surrounding planets were at war with each other. However, the planet Knob, with all its citizens, did not seem to be affected by the current war.

The storyteller sets the fundamental context in which the story unfolds. Notice that the planet, or home, is at peace, but the surrounding environment has some problems. The problems do not come from within but from the outside.

Knob's citizens were very happy. Their king treated them with fairness and justice. It was very important to the king that his kingdom remain that way. Therefore, he developed an excellent space force to protect his citizens from intruding warriors. That force included all kinds of spacecraft fighters, cruisers, and battleships.

Notice that the father image (king) is implicitly interpreted to be kind and good. Father does not place anyone under pressure.

Of course, the very best spacecraft was worthless without a well-trained spacecraft pilot at the controls. And so it was known throughout the galaxy that the king on Knob had the best-trained spaceship pilots. They flew their ships with unequaled skill and shot

Notice that the subject matter—spaceships, pilots, etc.—are likely to be of high interest for an eight-year-old boy. The story focuses on the well-trained and skilled pilot. Notice that the metaphor begins to draw a relationship between survival, peace, and a skilled pilot force (i.e., the more prepared, the better the chance at survival). The fact that the pilots on Knob are better prepared than anyone else is implied.

down any enemy ships that tried to penetrate their defense systems.

Many times, these battles came down to a real dogfight, but it was always the pilot of Knob who turned out to be the winner. The secret to this fabulous pilot-fighting force was in the way they were trained. Anyone could enter the training program, but only the best survived and passed the final flight tests. There were seven exams each pilot had to pass. Only if a pilot could pass the first exam was he permitted to take the next one—and so on, until all seven exams were successfully passed. This rigorous training method provided King Amod and his kingdom with excellent pilots for generations to come. The pilots, in fact, were so skilled that they were never shot down. They may have occasionally been injured or their spacecraft heavily damaged, but nobody was ever killed.

The metaphor further supports the above-introduced notion that training equals success. Notice that the metaphor alludes to the fact that Tom, by proper preparedness, can consider himself special, an elite. Now the metaphor begins to introduce the idea that certain basic skills have to be mastered before one can go on to the next task—a concept fundamental to the acquisition of scholastic or musical skills. Proper acquisition of skills is an insurance policy for success. Now, the stage has been set in which the characters (with which we hope Tom will identify) can be placed in the story context.

One day, Miro, a young pilot recruit, walked into the king's palace and said, "I want to become a pilot."

"Very well," said the king. "Go to the flight minister, and he will tell you what you must do."

The main character is introduced. It is with him, of course, that Tom will identify. The metaphor underscores the eagerness and enthusiasm of Miro, implying that the acquisition of new skills and knowledge is an exciting undertaking.

"Yes, sir," said Miro, and he marched off to see the flight minister.

The flight minister told Miro of all the different attack plans, defensive maneuvers, and the interceptive systems. He showed him the variety of spaceships and how they operated under different battle conditions. Then the flight minister explained to Miro about the seven different exams.

A sense of curiosity and excitement is created that reminds Tom of his very first encounters with learning experiences. All this helps Tom to identify with the metaphor, transforming himself into the fabric of the story.

The more the flight minister explained things to Miro, the more Miro became excited. "I can't wait!" he said to himself. "I can't wait to actually sit in one of these ships and let it rip." He could hardly sleep that night, and when the sun came up over the horizon, Miro put on his new uniform and was ready to go.

Helpers are introduced. These helpers may be any number of counterparts in Tom's life. They may be his parents or perhaps the piano teacher. The metaphor introduces the notion that life can be very complex but also incredibly intriguing at the same time.

He met two of his flight instructors that morning. They were very helpful in showing him how to operate the flight simulator. The things he had to learn were amazingly complex. There were so many buttons, levers, knobs, and handles, and it seemed like they all needed to be pushed or moved at the same time. Whenever he had a question or got lost, the two flight

By the same token, his parents, teachers, and many other people are always eager to help. Nobody likes to see someone get stuck in the process of learning. Learning can be an exhausting and rewarding experience.

instructors were right there to help him and get him back on track. That night, Miro could not believe how tired and exhausted he was. It did not take him but five seconds to fall asleep.

His training continued for about a week, and now the time had come for him to take the first of seven exams. The time had arrived for him to sit alone, without any help in the flight simulator. Miro could feel his heart pounding. It almost felt as if it would jump out of his chest. He noticed the sweat was slowly running down his forehead, and his hands were shaking as he took hold of the main control thruster.

Miro was scared. As a matter of fact, he was so fearful that he froze for a minute. Then he noticed how the thrust of the rapid acceleration pushed him back into his seat. Miro frantically tried to get his ship under control. He barely escaped an enemy battle cruiser who attempted to blow his ship apart.

Learning, practicing, and training—the acquisition of new skills is not an overnight phenomenon but takes time, commitment, and effort. Tom's anger about having to attempt new tasks is interpreted as fear of having to perform or fear of failure. Fear, in fact, can be a very emotionally consuming experience.

The reframe of the bridge is introduced. Anger and hostility are transformed into fear. This general fear of failure is taken one step further in its interpretation. It is explained as the fear of letting teachers and parents down. Fear of disappointing these people is not necessarily a bad thing. After all, if one has no fear, others would not feel respect for him, and having respect in general is a good thing.

For a moment, he thought of how awful it would be if he were to fail his first exam. The thought of disappointing his two flight instructors sent chills down his spine. Never had Miro been quite so overwhelmed and frightened. When the test was over, he realized he had passed—barely. He was relieved and quite exhausted.

Miro did not get much of a chance to relax. The very next day, training for the second exam started. It seemed even more difficult than the first. He still remembered vividly how scared and frightened he had been when he took the last exam. Miro said to himself, "I am not going to be scared like that again. This time I'm going to practice and train even more intently."

When time came to take the second exam, Miro was still scared, but he did not experience the same paralyzing fear he had before. This time, Miro didn't just barely pass—he passed by a wide margin.

As the training continued, Miro became less frightened and scared. His confidence grew, and when he

Another reframe is introduced. Namely, the fear is a motivator for practice and preparation. This kind of fear is certainly not bad, but in fact, useful. Sometimes, fear of failure turns out to be a motivating factor. It forces one to prepare effectively and, thus, approach new tasks with increased confidence.

This notion is reinforced here. As a result, the metaphoric bridge or reframe is expanded to the notion that anger is really fear, and in reality, is the desire to do well. In short, anger is the drive, desire, or motivation to perform up to the level of expectation.

The metaphor touches on the concept that practice, not giving up, and overcoming fear will eventually lead to success. Mastering a task is directly related to dedication to practice.

sat in the flight simulator, he pulled buttons and switches with fantastic accuracy and speed. Even his flight instructors were amazed by his ability to fly the spaceship with such skill.

The time had come for Miro to take the seventh and final exam. This exam was not to take place in the flight simulator but in a real spaceship under real battle conditions. It was a cold and windy morning on the planet. All the space cadets lined up to take their last flight instructions. The king himself wished the pilots well, and off they went.

Now the metaphor sets the stage for the final message. Even with practice, the real event is always different than anticipated. However, the time spent in preparation provides one with the confidence and experience to encounter the surprises in a successful way.

At first, Miro could not see any enemy spaceships, but then, all of a sudden, they appeared—not just one but six of them. Miro did not have time to be scared. He maneuvered his fighter ship up and down, in spirals and circles, and when it was all over, there was minor damage to his left wing. However, the enemy fighters were shot down.

The metaphor carries the message that fear is actually a lifesaver. Anger, reframed into fear, turned out to be a positive thing rather than a handicap. Notice that this notion is brought to a conclusion in the story. Tom's apparent anger was first reframed into fear of tackling new things. Then this fear was further reframed into the intense desire to do well and not to disappoint parents and teachers. Finally, fear turned out to be the very thing that taught Tom to succeed in the acquisition of new skills and knowledge.

On his way home, Miro realized that having been scared was the greatest thing that ever happened to him, because otherwise, he would not have been prepared for his seventh exam. When he approached the landing base, Miro saw hundreds of people awaiting the arrival of the new pilots. Everyone was proud of them. The king, standing on the platform, gave everyone a medal. "Well done. You've earned it," he said.

The story builds on the strategy of a reframe: turning anger into something positive and constructive. Drawing again on the situation of Tom, let us develop one more example of a metaphor. Again, we will utilize a reframe as a strategy or bridge.

METAPHOR

Some time ago, I read a very interesting story in a magazine. A family from Texas went skiing in Colorado. The primary reason for this was that their daughter, Heidi, begged her parents for months to take her skiing. Heidi had seen many pictures of snow-covered mountains and skiers moving down big, wide slopes. This was one of the most exciting things to do that Heidi could imagine. She was so anxious about wanting to ski. In fact, that was just about all Heidi could talk about.

She told all of her friends at school that she was going to be a good skier. Somehow, she knew she was

COMMENTARY

The storyteller sets the stage. Notice that the story is not a "tale" but simply a story in the here and now.

The task of skiing is the metaphoric representation of trying something new, such as playing the piano or any other new task Tom is faced with.

The beginning of the reframe is set up as the undertaking of a new task. It is exciting and not frightening.

Seeking one's peers' approval is always a part of mastering any new task. The element of pride is introduced. One cannot let others down going to glide down those slopes with the greatest elegance. Failure never entered her mind. Her friends knew it too.

The time had finally come. Heidi and her parents left for Colorado and spent the first day with a ski instructor. Everybody made great progress. On the second day, the family progressed to the bunny hill. Mom began first, then Dad followed, and Heidi was not far behind. All of a sudden, Heidi fell spread eagle. With snow all over her face—in her ears, mouth, and nose—she stood up. Heidi was mad. She threw her ski poles halfway down the mountain, sat in the snow, took her skis off, and said, "I've had it. This is ridiculous. If you think that I'm going to punish myself by falling all the way down the mountain, you're wrong!"

Her parents did not pay any great attention to her antics and skied down the hill. At the lodge, they unstrapped their skis and waited. They figured that talking to Heidi while she was mad would probably be a fruitless effort. They decided to give her the chance to work through her emotions herself.

once a promise has been made. The idea of being on top of things and looking good is paramount for any child.

Skiing down the slopes is the metaphoric representation of approaching a new and novel task.

Again, the metaphor should be a short story, and any skillful storyteller will need to elaborate, following the principle of using "flowery language."

The stage is set for the reframe. First, the idea is introduced that the real task is always harder than anticipated. The actual follow-through of a new task is often different from the idea itself.

Secondly, to be angered by an accident is certainly not unusual. Falling down when learning how to ski is perfectly acceptable, and after all, who would not become a little testy about having a snow-covered face. Metaphorically, the child is told that he must work this out for

Heidi, still atop the mountain, was steaming with anger. Her red face glowed like a light bulb against the background of her white parka and the snow. She sat there for at least an hour. As the time passed, she realized that there was only one way to get off that mountain. Reluctantly, she snapped her skis back on. After all, she was not about to let her friends laugh at her by going home from her trip as anything less than an expert.

At about that same time, a ski instructor came by. Assessing the situation rather quickly, he asked Heidi, "Have you noticed how your knees are shaking?" Heidi got angrier but had to agree that her entire body was shaking. Jake, the ski instructor, said, "You know, being scared is a wonderful thing. It keeps people from getting killed on these steep slopes. Once in a while, we get a hotshot who comes up here and thinks he can mow right down these slopes. You know what? It never fails. Those guys always end up in the hospital or in a cast, wondering what went wrong."

From Heidi's conversation with the ski instructor, she gained a new outlook on skiing. The discovery

himself. Nobody can do it for him. One can assist him, but ultimately, he has to perform the task.

Third, the reframe is further developed by introducing the notion that behind the anger, there are possibly many different emotions, such as the disappointment from falling and the fear of failure.

An appeal is made to the person's pride. The desire to do well in the presence of one's peers can indeed be a motivating force.

Metaphorically, the listener is told that it is perfectly permissible to take advice from those with experience. Taking tips from parents or teachers may in fact facilitate the learning process and help overcome obstacles.

Now, the idea is introduced that fear can be a great emotion. We have reframed anger into disappointment and disappointment into fear. We explain why fear can be useful. Fear is a tempering device. It assists the person with placing an optimal amount of energy into the undertaking of a task. Fear is a bridle that can actually enhance learning.

The listener is told that one learns from learning. It is not an end in itself that fear might actually make her a better skier was a revelation. Not having to be a hotshot and prove to her friends how good she was lifted a great burden from her mind. Over time, as she improved her skiing, the task became easier and Heidi learned much faster.

but a process that unlocks other doors of knowledge and insight.

The strategies of encouragement and reframing are certainly two very important bridges one may utilize getting the listener from the problem to a resolution. By no means, however, do these strategies represent all the available ways of showing the child the way. In fact, there are as many options available as the imagination of the story-teller. The possibilities are endless. After all, there are many ways to skin a cat.

CHAPTER 10

more ways to skin a cat

We have learned that an effective story is built around a strategy. The strategy is a bridge that allows a listener to cross from problematic thoughts and behaviors to more effective practices. This chapter will introduce additional strategies that address a listener's particular needs.

Unite and Conquer

Most parents are familiar with a child who has difficulty abandoning troublesome behaviors. To the bewilderment of the well-meaning parent, a child may want to hang on to poor behaviors or maladaptive thought patterns and reject any help for overcoming them. The word stubborn is fitting—an unwillingness to admit there is a problem, which is manifested through the familiar refrain of, "You just don't understand."

Such a situation may call for the "Unite and Conquer" strategy.

Henry is adamant that there is nothing wrong with pestering and pushing his younger sister when things do not go his way. Both parents have talked with him repeatedly about the inappropriateness of his behavior. Henry is of the opinion that he has every right to shove his sister if she does not return his toys when he wants them back. His parents have talked to him to the point of exhaustion. More often than not, as soon as Henry suspects his mother or father of lecturing him, he responds in a most apathetic fashion. Quite often, his parents indicate that their advice has the appearance of going in one ear and out the other.

It is evident that Henry has developed a deaf ear to direct parental intervention methods, as he has been lectured repetitively, responding with "auditory closure." The following metaphor utilizes the "Unite and Conquer" strategy as the basis for the story.

As you remember, Henry, last year, Mother and I went to visit Uncle John in Michigan. While we were there, a very interesting thing happened to us. We were sitting on the beach one day, and along came a group of children and some adults. We thought they were probably with a school or some other youth group. Your mom and I noticed right away that one of the boys was noticeably smaller than the other children. As he dragged somewhat behind the group, he played with a small dog. The little dog looked like a stray and enjoyed running around the beach.

The boy continued to play with the dog, which barked a few times and then jumped on the boy. It looked as though the stray dog had found a friend. The boy picked up a stick and threw it as far as he could. As the stick fell to the ground, the dog chased after it. This play between the dog and the boy lasted only a short time, as the boy grew tired of playing with the dog.

Soon, the boy kicked the dog. The dog whined and ran away a short distance, but after a while, the dog came right back to play some more. It was obvious that the dog did not understand the boy was tired of playing with him. As soon as the dog got back to the boy, I could not believe it; the boy kicked the dog again. By now, the screeching dog had caught the attention of one of the adults in the group. This gentleman shook his head and mumbled, "That's Ron. He's always picking on things that really can't hurt him back."

One of the other adults overheard the gentleman's comments and said, "The fact that Ron has a need to pick on somebody (or something) smaller shows that he is really a weakling. All weaklings pick on weaker targets to help make themselves feel better. In reality, you can often spot weaklings because they pick on people that can't or don't reciprocate."

You will have recognized that this particular metaphor was not of the "classic form" variety but followed the criteria of the "statement form." Again, the direct approach of addressing Henry's problem is disguised in the metaphor. The statement form metaphor disguises the direct approach equally well. Resistance is reduced because the parents discussed a boy and a dog and are not lecturing their son through the process. You will have also noticed that the requirements of fitting life characters with those of the metaphor have also been met. Henry will very likely identify himself with the boy in the story.

Disguised through the metaphor, the parent proposes to Henry the "real" reason for the aggressing behavior toward his sister—taking advantage of somebody that can't defend herself. Even Henry will agree that taking advantage of a weaker person is not appropriate. He may argue that his sister is the cause of his aggression. However, the metaphor of the story reduces such an argument. After all, we are talking about a boy and a dog. Moreover, the story links aggressive behaviors with being weak. The only way for Henry to deny that he is weak is to discontinue harassing his sister.

Another example will help add perspective to this particular strategy.

Eleven-year-old Heather has chronic problems with completing her homework. She conveniently forgets, makes excuses, and insists that she has no homework. Her parents have talked with her many times about the importance of completing homework. They tell her how tired they are of having to prod her all the time and repeatedly encourage Heather to demonstrate more responsibility by doing her homework without being asked. It seems that the more her parents encourage and prod Heather, the less she is willing to comply.

A metaphor utilizing the "Unite and Conquer" strategy may take the following format:

Heather, watching these ice-skating competitions on television reminds me of someone I once knew. Mark and I went to the same high school. I think he was a senior when I was a sophomore. Mark was always good at ice skating. Not only was he the best skater we had on our ice hockey team but also his ice-skating routine—you know the kind we've been watching on TV—was unbelievable. He won every trophy possible. Then, all of a sudden, an interesting thing happened. When it came time for the state championship, he refused to participate. Fellow students and teachers who knew him were very upset over the fact that he refused to play. But Mark insisted, and that was it. He was going to hang up his skates. You can well imagine that everyone wanted to know why? "Why would you want to quit, Mark?" they asked.

Mark insisted that he was not interested anymore. At times, he even indicated that he hated skating. Everyone was in shock, and many asked, "What's happening with Mark?" Nobody seemed to be able to come up with a good explanation.

Years later, I ran into Liz, his old girlfriend from high school. Of course, we started to chat about Mark, and then she went on to tell me of the letters she received about the time he refused to skate in the state championship. Liz said that back then, Mark told her he was scared to skate in front of all of those people. He was horrified by the idea that he could fall and lose the game. Liz said, "It wasn't really that he hated to skate. Sadly, he was just afraid of success. Success demands a lot of someone. You have to keep it up. You can't feel a little lazy one day, or else your game goes downhill." That was his way out, I guess.

Like the previous metaphor, this story follows the statement form. The strategy is based on the notion that hating and refusing to do homework is, in reality, nothing more than a fear of success. Hence, in order for the child to reject the idea that it is not the fear of success that keeps her from doing her homework, she also has to reject the idea that she does not hate homework. Again, this message is hidden in the metaphor and a confrontation between parent and child is less likely to occur. After all, it's just a story.

The "Unite and Conquer" strategy lends itself particularly well to situations when an undesirable behavior of a child needs to be eliminated—and the child, for whatever reason, appears to have a great need to hang on to the inappropriate behavior. In situations like these, we are not concerned with the acquisition of a new skill or behavior but seek to be rid of maladaptive behaviors. A final example will illustrate this point once more.

Barry's bad language has become more and more disrespectful. A few weeks prior, eleven-year-old Barry began using certain four-letter words. At first his parents tried to ignore him and hoped he was going through a phase. But what they hoped was a temporary habit soon turned into constant embarrassment. Barry's parents' attempts to reason with him, telling him that such language is uncouth, offensive, and intolerable, did not work. On a few occasions, Barry was sent to his room, and he has been repeatedly grounded for his behavior.

Just when Barry's parents started to believe things had settled down, they discovered from neighboring parents and children that the bad language had never stopped. Here is a possible story:

In the Old West, prior to the arrival of the first white men, the land was dotted with Indian tribes. Many were nomadic people.

They were always on the move, looking for animals they could hunt. When they had settled down for a while in one spot and killed many of the animals, soon they had to move on to look for new hunting grounds. The majority of them lived in tents, which allowed them to quickly move from place to place.

The women prepared all the food and did all the cooking. They also made the clothing. The men were hunters and warriors. They were responsible for bringing home the meat and protecting the tribe from attacks. Not all the tribes were the same. Some were peaceful and others were continually on the warpath, looking to steal horses from other tribes—in some cases, even stealing their women. Those particular Indians painted their faces and often painted their ponies, too. When they attacked the camp of another tribe, they yelled and screamed in hopes of intimidating their opponents. Their most fearsome weapon was the lance. It could be used to kill an enemy from a distance, avoiding hand-to-hand combat.

The Indians had no written history. The only "written" pieces we have of them are the paintings and signs on rock walls. However, they had a vast oral history. When the white men came to this land, many of these oral histories and legends were recorded and written in books. One of these is the legend of Running Horse, the mighty hunter.

Running Horse (of course this is not the name he was first known as) was first known as Little Mouse. In the Indian village where Little Mouse grew up, there were six families who had boys about the same age as Little Mouse. Like most children, they played together. They made clay figures, used paint to draw animals on cloth, and *played a game that is known today as lacrosse. As they grew older, their play involved hunting games. One of the boys would pretend to be a buffalo, and the other boys would chase him down, jump on him, and wrestle him to the ground. Other times, a boy would pretend to be a prairie dog and would hide as the other boys chased. While this was a lot of fun, the boys knew some day the games would become real. In a way, the games provided early training for them to take their rightful place among the hunters of the tribe. But for now, it was all fun.*

As the boys played their hunting games, it became increasingly apparent that Little Mouse was not as strong and skilled as some of the other young Indian boys. He was smaller, weighed less, and couldn't run as fast—nor was he quite as agile as the others.

Secretly, Little Mouse was disappointed in himself and pondered a great deal about how he could catch up to the other Indian boys. He was very worried that, perhaps, he wouldn't grow up to be the mighty hunter he ultimately wished to become. Little Mouse spent many hours by himself, wondering what he could possibly do to become as quick and powerful as the other boys.

Then, suddenly, he had an idea. He was going to impress his friends, no matter the cost. He planned to sneak into the camp of the tribe that lived on the other side of the mountain and steal a lance from one of the warriors. The tribe of Little Mouse were hunters, using only bows and arrows. They did not use lances. Lances were only used by warriors to attack other Indian villages. If he could show up with one of those feared lances, then the other Indian boys would respect him. And so Little Mouse left his tent in the middle of the night, crossed the mountain, and snuck into the camp of the neighboring tribe, where he stole a lance that was leaning next to a tent. He knew that he should not possess the stolen lance, but his desire to impress his friends was greater.

The next morning, Little Mouse couldn't wait to parade the lance in front of everybody. All the boys seemed impressed. Little Mouse felt that he had finally measured up to the other boys. His parents, on the other hand, had absolutely no tolerance for allowing their boy to carry a lance. They knew he had stolen it from another tribe, so they insisted that he dispose of the lance. Little Mouse protested. He did not want to part with his newly acquired lance and popularity.

Little Mouse did not know what to do. On the one hand, he was convinced he had finally impressed the other boys, while on the other hand, his parents insisted that he get rid of the very thing that provided him with this new respect he so desperately sought. Then he had an idea. He would hide the lance from his parents. During the day, however, while he and the other boys played their hunting games, he would retrieve the lance. This way, his parents would believe he had gotten rid of the lance and his friends would continue to be impressed.

One day he was walking behind a teepee and overheard some of the boys talking about the lance. He heard one boy say, "The lance is fearsome, but Little Mouse is still Little Mouse." Little Mouse felt very bad. Could it be possible that the other boys were impressed with the lance but not with him? He thought about that question all night long. The more he thought about it, the less he knew what to do.

The next day, Little Mouse went to the teepee of the medicine man. He told him all about the boys making fun of him and about him stealing the lance to impress them. Little Mouse also told him about what he had overheard as the boys talked about him and the lance.

The medicine man, with his legs folded, sat quietly on a woven blanket. The few sunrays that found themselves through the top of the teepee illuminated his old face. He took some magic powder out of a pouch and threw some of it in the small fire in front of him. He held the rest of the magic power in the palm of his right hand. Then he spit in that same hand and mixed the saliva with the magic powder and rubbed the mixture on the forehand, arms, and legs of Little Mouse. After that he spoke. "Return lance and come back Running Horse. Now, go!" That's all he said. Little Mouse understood that the medicine man wanted him to return the lance, but he had no idea what he meant by saying, "Come back Running Horse."

The next evening, Little Mouse took the lance, snuck out of his teepee, and headed for the Indian tribe across the mountain. He reached their camp at daybreak. As he carefully put the lance back where he had taken it from, some dogs noticed him and barked. Suddenly, there was shouting and screaming. Knife and tomahawk in hand, warriors emerged from their teepees, looking around to find who or what had intruded their camp.

Little Mouse was lightning fast. He took off running. Never in his life had he run so fast. He kept running and running. Even when he thought he couldn't run any farther, he kept running. When he felt that his legs couldn't carry him anymore, he kept running. When he felt that his lungs would collapse at any second, he kept running.

Meanwhile, at daybreak his family noticed Little Mouse was missing. By asking around the camp, they found out from the medicine man that he had left to return the lance. Many in the camp were worried about Little Mouse, wondering if he would return safely.

By midmorning, they could see him appearing on the crest of a nearby hill. He was running. He was running faster than a horse. Everybody in the camp knew what had happened. They knew that Little Mouse was discovered by the warrior tribe while returning the lance, but little Mouse escaped by running faster than a horse.

That day, the Indian tribe changed his name to Running Horse, and eventually he took his rightful place as a mighty hunter among his people.

Let us briefly examine the elements of this metaphor. The pertinent building blocks include the following:

- The story follows the classic form in that a person encounters a problem but somehow or someway overcomes the obstacle.

- The story takes place among Indian tribes, a context that an eleven-year-old, pre-pubescent boy will appreciate.

- The story does not immediately dive into the essential cast of characters but adds them as needed. By doing so, the listener's anticipation is heightened, which will likely increase attention to what is being told.

- The transformation of Little Mouse to Running Horse is introduced from the beginning. As the story is told, the listener knows in advance that such a positive transformation is forthcoming, which reinforces the anticipation of how it is going to happen.

- The Indian names of Little Mouse and Running Horse are strategically chosen. They underline the metaphoric transformation of turning inferiority into competence.

- The lance is the undesirable behavior—in this case, the foul and unacceptable language.

- The story communicates the notion that the lance (bad language) is not part of the make-up of the Indian tribe in which Little Mouse lives.

- The strategy is accomplished by linking bad language with immaturity. In essence, the story portrays the notion that bad language is a cover-up for immaturity, a combination that the listener abhors. After all, what pre-pubescent boy wants to be labeled immature?

- The medicine man provides the opportunity to reverse the link of bad language and immaturity for a new combination—courage to give up something negative and harvest something good: respect.

CHAPTER 11

some more strategies

In previous chapters, we introduced a number of strategies to connect children with insightful metaphors, the core around which the story is built. In this chapter, we will introduce two additional strategies that utilize a paradoxical approach to help motivate the troubled child. Paradoxical approaches are methods that utilize the misbehavior in such a fashion that the child feels prompted to give it up—without "demanding" of the child to surrender the misbehavior.

Turning the Tables

The "Turning the Tables" strategy operates along the same underlying principles as the fairy tale of the Frog Prince. This tale conveys the message that by overcoming oneself, the repulsive, or by embracing that which is falsely despised, one can indeed obtain great rewards.

An example will illustrate:

Most people who know fourteen-year-old Jennifer agree that she is very bright. When she is willing to put her effort into a project, she is typically successful. The problem is that she has few or no friends. For reasons unknown to her, her peers show little interest. Jennifer has had a few relationships; however, they've been superficial or haven't endured. She is discouraged and has withdrawn. To her peers, however, she shows increasing intolerance and at times comes across as angry and aloof. There are two girls in particular with whom Jennifer desires to become friends, but for some reason, those friendships never materialize, much to Jennifer's disappointment. Her parents suspect that her peers, and particularly those two girls, are intimidated or simply jealous of Jennifer's intelligence.

Before we respond to the above situation with a metaphor, let us consider briefly the typical or traditional approach to helping Jennifer solve her problem. In most situations, the approach to her problem may include a lecture with language such as, "Your intelligence is intimidating your friends, and you should do something different to make friends." Most fourteen-year-old children would likely respond to this approach with defensiveness. Wrapping basic concern and observation, along with a possible solution, in the disguise of a metaphor is far more promising. Here is a possible metaphor.

Many years ago, when the unicorn still roamed the plains of what is now known as Northern Europe, there was a group of people who lived near the Baltic Sea. They were a small group, but their power was great. This was not power of military might and prowess. These people possessed personal power—the power of confidence and wisdom. There were many ways and means in which these people attained such powers ... through old customs that had existed longer than anyone could remember.

One particular ancient custom was that each time a baby was born, a fairy would visit the newborn child. The birthday fairy, as she was called, would bestow each new baby with a gift. As each child was born, the birthday fairy appeared and laid the chosen birthday gift next to the bed of each baby. The gifts came in many different shapes and sizes. Some were small and some were big. There were those that were very colorful, while others looked rather plain. Some gifts were simple in design, but others were more complicated. Some had immediate practical use for the newborn baby, while others gave the initial impression of being worthless. Of course, the views changed with the age of the child who received a particular gift. Some of these gifts were not discovered by the child until later in life so that the gift took on practical use after each child grew older. Thus, there were gifts that, to a small child, appeared of little use. However, as the child grew older, these gifts became more valuable and meaningful.

No two children ever received the same gift. The gifts were not transferable; they could neither be exchanged with the gifts of other children, nor could they be traded. So it was with Elsha, the youngest child of Vor and Ilse. When the day of her birth came, the birthday fairy bestowed her with a most beautiful gift. It did not take long for other children to notice Elsha's exquisite gift. It was a small golden box and was most magnificent. The box sparkled and was covered with many precious stones, such as diamonds, rubies, sapphires, and pearls. When other children of the village came to play, they noticed Elsha's beautiful box, and she soon became accustomed to showing her precious box all over the village. "Let me have the box," said one child. "I wish I had a beautiful box like that," said another. Wherever Elsha went, the children wanted to see her golden box.

It was not unusual for some children to want to see and even touch the box more than once. Many children who had seen the box wished that they, too, could have the box. For many, a desire for the box often turned to envy, causing many children to turn away from Elsha, as they had become jealous. At one time, she had many visitors who wanted to see her box, but now she often sat home alone.

At first, Elsha was saddened by the other children's reactions, but she grew determined that she was not going to sit around the home alone, while other children played with each other. And so it came about that Elsha proudly displayed her box in front of the other children. "See my beautiful box," she said to one child. "Wouldn't you like to have such a box?"

One day, while Elsha paraded her golden box in front of the children, she heard a small voice come from within it. At first Elsha was terrified, but eventually she mustered enough courage to open the box. No sooner had she opened it than a tiny man with a long red beard and a huge nose jumped out and instantly turned into a giant. He took the coiled rope, hanging from his belt, tied her hands, blindfolded her eyes, and took her prisoner to his underground castle, where he promptly threw her into a dungeon. Completely left alone, the only visitors she had were rats and the daily visits from one of the ugly monsters, who laughed at her with a horribly deep voice as he brought regular meals of bread and water.

At first, Elsha was very angry with the other children for making her show them her box, but soon her anger turned to despair. She grew sad and lonely. The hard wooden bed in her prison cell would not allow her to sleep well, and each morning she woke up sadder and more hopeless. She fought back tears, but finally Elsha could not keep them back any longer. Sitting on the edge of her shabby bed with tears running down her cheeks, she pulled the fateful golden box out of her pocket. As she held the box in her shaky little hands, a tear fell onto the box. No sooner had the tear touched the box than the birthday fairy appeared. "How can I help you, child?" inquired the fairy in her warm and tender tone. Elsha told the sad story to the birthday fairy.

"I will help you," declared the fairy. "In the afternoon, when the ugly, red-bearded giant takes his afternoon nap, I will sneak you out of the castle. Then I will take you to your friends, at which point you

must inquire about their gifts. Each night, I will have to take you back to the dungeon."

At first, Elsha did not see how those afternoon trips to her friends could possibly help free her from the binds of the giant, but trustingly, she followed the directions of the birthday fairy. The first afternoon Elsha went to one friend and inquired about her gift by asking how the gift was put to use. The time went quickly and she found herself back at her prison cell, where the big red-bearded giant had prepared supper. She asked herself, "Could it be that I am just imagining this, or is the giant smaller than he normally is? No," she said, "it's just my imagination."

The next afternoon Elsha went with the birthday fairy to see another friend. Again, she inquired about her friend's gift, wanting to know all about it and asking many questions. Elsha noticed that her friend smiled at her. However, before she had been taken prisoner, the same friend had avoided her. Like the day before, the afternoon passed very quickly, and Elsha returned in time for the regular evening meal of bread and water. Now, it was not just her imagination. There was no question about it. The giant was smaller. He was not as big as he had been just two days before.

With each successive day, Elsha spent much of her time with different children from the village, inquiring about their gifts. She was astonished by the diversity of gifts the other children possessed. Each day a different friend welcomed her, and each friend was saddened when Elsha had to leave for the dungeon. Equally astonishing was the fact that the giant continued to become smaller each day.

And so the day came when Elsha could reach between the iron rods of her prison door, pick up the giant who had become a little man, and put him back in her golden box. No sooner had she put the lid back on the box than the spell was broken. Elsha found herself back with her family in the village on the Baltic Sea, and she lived happily ever after, knowing that all gifts are significant.

Through the example, we are able to recognize the essential elements that make this metaphor functional:

- Jennifer identifies with our heroine, Elsha.

- The story is presented in the classic form.

- The gifts are representative of Jennifer's skills, intelligence, and abilities. For that matter, the gifts represent all the diversified talents given to each child.

- By boasting those skills, one has a tendency to get out of control and, as a result, gifts may become deficits rather than assets. The giant represents this idea metaphorically.

- The monster, however, can be controlled and eventually put away in direct relationship to paying attention to other people's talents, skills, and accomplishments. In short, "What goes around comes around."

If You Can't Beat 'Em, Join 'Em!

This bridge is very simple yet can be extremely powerful in the right situation. Most parents have dealt with a young child who is so upset that he or she declares: "I'm going to run away." Rather than discussing the ill consequences of running away, the clever mother promptly announces, "John, I realize how terrible you have it here, and I wouldn't blame you for running away. In fact, let me get the suitcase for you. I'll make you a nice sack lunch for your trip."

Parents who employ such strategies are confident that the child will not run away. Rather than confronting or trying to convince the child of ill-construed and ridiculous plans, the parent not only agrees but suggests steps for accomplishing the task, thereby making the situation even more ridiculous, almost humorous. Hence, the strategy of "joining" rather than fighting.

Frank is rapidly approaching the age of sixteen. The idea of having a "set of wheels" appears to have taken over every cell in his brain. The earnings from his part-time job are used to purchase car magazines. In fact, Frank has subscribed to three different titles. His weekends are spent on the showroom floors of different car dealerships.

His parents agree that perhaps an older used car may be within their budget, but a new car is out of the question. Frank does not see it that way. The frequent phone calls from car salesmen are beginning to annoy his parents. Both his mother and father, aware of their financial resources, have attempted to talk Frank out of his utopian ideas, but they have been rather unsuccessful. Frank's dream of owning a new car has taken on the form of ridiculousness. But Frank is not responding very well to common sense. Parental pleas and logic are met with the following response: "Why are you being so negative about this? You are simply refusing to see it my way."

The fact is that there are too many fancy, new cars speeding around in Frank's head. A metaphorical approach, as in the following example, is required.

Once upon a time in a country far, far away, there lived a farmer and his family. They lived near the woods, where the farmer had cleared enough trees to make room for wheat and cornfields. They had a vegetable garden and a few cattle. The farmer and his wife had many children. They all enjoyed working on the farm, and playing hide-and-seek in the nearby woods was one of their favorite pastimes.

One day, Jack, the oldest son, went for a walk in the forest by himself and for the first time noticed all the different wild animals. It was exciting. Jack had great fun in the forest and returned many times to observe the wildlife. And so it came about that Jack spent more and more time in the forest. He became so enchanted with all the forest creatures that farming did not appeal to him any longer. Farming, raising wheat, corn, and other vegetables was simply too boring when compared to the idea of hunting wild animals. Jack wanted to be a hunter. He gathered his savings and went into town, where he purchased a beautiful hunting rifle before heading off into the woods.

When Jack had that first rabbit in his sight, his whole body trembled with excitement. It was hard for him to hold the rifle still. Just when he was about to pull the trigger, from the corner of his eye came a fox. The fox was beautiful. His golden, red coat gleamed in the sun. "Why bother with a little rabbit, if you can have a fox?" he said to himself. Jack quickly took aim on the fox. His hands trembled with anticipation, and it was difficult for him to get his breathing under control. When he finally had the fox in sight, he could not help noticing a deer standing in the clearing just a few feet behind the fox. Frank was torn. "Should I shoot the fox or try to get the deer?" he asked himself. "Of course, everyone will be much more impressed with a deer than a measly fox."

Once the debate in Frank's mind had come to an end, the deer was gone. But that did not stop Frank. He continued beyond the clearing and on the other side, on top of a little knoll, he spotted a wild boar. "Anyone can shoot a deer," Frank said, "but a wild boar is something entirely different." This time Frank did not hesitate. He quickly took aim. As soon as he had a good look at the boar, he saw the antlers of what must have been an enormous elk. "Now, that's a trophy," he said. Quickly, Frank aimed and fired. But when he got to where the elk stood, there was no animal to be found. As mysteriously as the elk had appeared, it had disappeared, and the echo of the boom from his shot reached the ears of every wild animal in the forest.

Frank was a little embarrassed when he came home without a trophy. His younger brothers and sisters laughed, but his mother and father knew what a frustrating day Frank must have experienced in the forest. They took him into their arms and gave him a heartfelt hug.

- This metaphor encourages the recipient to pursue an idea, even if it is ridiculous.

- In addition, there is the notion that if you "want to endlessly pursue the bigger and the better" option, you may end up with nothing.

Here is another metaphor that applies to the same situation, utilizing the same strategy, which may look like this:

Jack had a very peculiar dream. He dreamt he was in a big restaurant with hunger the size of China. He sat down at a table, and a nice, big, juicy, steaming hot dog appeared. Jack picked it up, and just when he was ready to take a bite, a little old man appeared.

"Jack, a young man like you with an appetite the size of an elephant should not waste your time on a hot dog. After all, an appetite like yours deserves better," the little old man said. And with that, he disappeared.

"Now, there's a man who really understands," Jack said. He put down the hot dog and looked around the room for bigger and better food.

He walked over to another table and really liked what he saw. There was the biggest burger he had ever seen, with all the trimmings. The smell of french fries drove him wild. He picked the burger up, and again, the little old man appeared.

"Jack, a man like you should not be satisfied with a common, ordinary burger. A burger like that should not be wasted on an appetite like yours."

Jack agreed. He was so hungry he could hardly stand it. He knew there was finally somebody who understood the magnitude of his hunger. And so, Jack looked around the room for another table.

And sure enough, in the corner sat a plate with a thick juicy steak, mashed potatoes, vegetables, a hot roll with butter, jam, and a slice of chocolate cake. Jack could hardly stand it. His eyes jumped out of his head. His tongue touched his chin, and saliva dripped from every gland in his mouth. Of course, just about then, the little old man appeared.

"You know, Jack, this looks pretty good, but a man with your appetite deserves better."

Jack had had it. As he was ready to take a big bite out of that steak sitting before him, he woke up. The dream was over—the steak dinner was gone. Jack headed for the refrigerator, searching for anything edible.

Both metaphors encourage the child to pursue with an uncontrollable appetite. However, the story also alludes to the pitfalls of overzealous attempts to obtain the best, the biggest, and the most elaborate. Of course, the child may respond with such comments as, "I know what you are trying to do." Remember, this approach helps you to avoid getting trapped in a direct argument about whether or not the idea is outrageous. It is Frank's business to decide how he wants to interpret the metaphor.

You are merely telling a story.

CHAPTER 12

ignoring the bridge

In previous chapters, we introduced a number of different strategies. We labeled these Encouragement, Reframing, Unite and Conquer, Turning Tables, and If you Can't Beat 'Em, Join 'Em. We referred to these approaches as bridges, allowing a listener to cross from the troubled side to a safer side.

These strategies do not represent all possibilities that utilize a story or metaphor to assist a child in overcoming a problem or resolving an impasse. In fact, the possibilities are endless and are only restricted by the imagination of the storyteller.

The No-Strategy Strategy

It is important to understand that the metaphor without a particular strategy can be useful just the same. In other words, the metaphor, itself, can provide the necessary bridge to help the child cross from a problem to a resolution. The "No-Strategy" strategy operates on the notion that no interpretation of the problem, its origin, or how it is perpetuated is necessary for the metaphor to be effective. In the no-strategy metaphor, the presenting problem is metaphorically told, and correspondingly, a solution is offered. That solution may be presented in simple terms or through magic resolution. Finding the bridge from problem to resolution is up to the child. This strategy relies on the notion that the solution to the problem is inside the child. When offered the possibility that the problem can be overcome, the child will invent the solution.

An example will illustrate:

Max, a high school junior, has begun a disturbing trend. His parents have noticed that he routinely criticizes all of his teachers. Such criticisms are mainly directed at the methodology of the teachers' classroom communication. In essence, Max is at odds with their individual and collective professional judgments as the teachers interact with a host of different students, including Max. It is obvious that this criticism is affecting him adversely. Instead of focusing on his work and doing the best he can, he is overly concerned with the "inadequate" professional judgment of his teachers. These judgments have had a negative effect on his grades and his general emotional health. Max has turned into a Monday morning quarterback, much to the concern of his parents. They have talked to their son about this matter but feel Max responds to them much like he responds to his teachers. Here, then, is a possible metaphor that may help Max.

Each year, up little Cottonwood Canyon—east of Salt Lake City—one of the greatest events of technical climbing takes place. Climbers from all over the world gather at the west wall of the nine-storied Cliff Lodge to test their skills, not against each other but against the merciless clock. These are speed climbers. Their objective is simple: get to the top faster than anyone else.

These climbers are not "weekend warriors" who seek cheap thrills in relief of their mundane jobs. These men and women are pros. Through endless practice, exercising, and physical and mental conditioning, they have become the best at what they do. The way in which they climb a rock face propels audience members to view them as magicians, though they are far from it.

There is nothing magical about what they do. There are no smoke-and-mirror tricks that create an illusion for the observers standing below. The climbers make it to the top of that Cliff Lodge wall with strength, technique, courage, and above all, judgment. Yes, you heard me right, judgment.

Every one of these professionals faces that wall with a multiplicity of choices before them. You see, there are a host of hand and footholds available to choose from. Every time one of those climbers reaches for a new hold, he chooses from many options. But the one that he eventually chooses is, in his best judgment, the very best choice. Ultimately, the climber who arrives at the top of the wall the quickest—without falling—wins.

You would think that this relatively small group of top climbers from all over the world would pick the same route, time and time again, but that is not so. Not only do they vary in their approaches, but each individual climber also chooses a different route depending on the circumstances. For example, the same climber will use a specific approach route if the air is very humid, causing the hand or footholds to be slippery. The handhold that worked great on a sunny, dry day in autumn is the wrong one to rely on when it's a cold, soggy spring day.

What makes each of these climbers the very best at what they do is that they make the wisest decisions in the moment, depending on the conditions with which they are faced. Remember, the condition is often not their choosing. They cannot influence weather. They don't control the moisture or content of the air. Hence, they make continuous judgments about the options and conditions they face. Yet, even the best judgments, while under the pressure of finding the perfect route under difficult circumstances, do not guarantee the absence of complications. Even the best climbers on Cliff Lodge run into problems, though they do not bring them on themselves. They simply make the best judgments available to each—that day, that hour, that minute, that second. Moreover, a climber who is six-foot-four-inches tall typically takes a different route than a climber who is four-foot-eleven-inches tall. The very same spacing of hand and footholds present different challenges for different climbers. Hence, circumstances call for diverse decision-making strategies.

Much of these decision-making strategies escape the casual observer standing at the base of the Cliff Lodge. To study each climber on his or her way up, observing one's techniques, individual challenges, and route choice often escapes the amateur who has never attempted to climb a sheer rock wall. Only those spectators who attempt to duplicate what they have seen begin to understand the variables that are at stake in the highly skilled sport of speed climbing.

The example story includes no attempt to interpret Max's motivation to criticize his teachers. As a result, the story provides him with a bridge to direct his behavior on a more productive path. The metaphor simply provides a framework of the type of tasks teachers face on a daily basis. The metaphor leaves it up to Max to react in a more positive way. Of course, the backdoor approach offered (through the metaphor) significantly reduces the resistance Max may normally employ as he considers alterative reactions to his perceived problem. In summary, the metaphor simply invites Max to view the problem through the eyes of his teachers. Seeing a problem through the eyes of a perceived "antagonist" stands a better chance for resolving such issues.

The no-strategy approach can also be effective when the reason for a problem is obvious to the parent and perhaps to the child; however, the child will not, or cannot, "reveal" the true reason for the impasse for fear the parent may discover a weakness in the child. An example will illustrate:

Oliver, a fourth grader, is a delight to his beloved teachers. At parent-teacher conferences, his parents learn that he is bright, involves himself in class discussions, and follows through in a timely fashion with homework. He is considered the top student in his class—a gifted child. Oliver looks forward to going to school and talks to his parents about school happenings. When he and his parents move to a different part of the city Oliver is enrolled in a special class for gifted students. They notice that Oliver appears less enthusiastic since attending this new class. His mother is shocked when he announces one morning that he does not want to go to school. It is obvious that something is wrong.

After meeting with Oliver's new teacher, his parents find out that he is no longer the "top cat" and that he is getting some stiff competition from fellow schoolmates. In a conversation with Oliver, his parents quickly notice that he blames his lack of enthusiasm for school on a "stupid" teacher. The harsh reality that other students are equally, or perhaps even more capable, is difficult for Oliver to swallow. Hence, he resorts to what most people do, blaming one's own problems on somebody else. A possible metaphor may be as follows:

Many hundred years ago, on the steppe of what is now Mongolia, lived nomadic people. Because of their way of life, they were unusually skilled in the art and tricks of how to handle horses. They were herdsmen, and when they moved to new grazing grounds, they packed their tents and all other gear on horses. They also used the horses to herd their flocks. There were no fences, and the grazing area was extremely large. The only way they could keep their flocks together was to continuously round them up from their horses. Thus, they were very dependent on their horses. Almost every day, each citizen spent a considerable amount of time in the saddle.

Because much of their life depended on being good horsemen, all the boys and girls learned to handle horses at an early age, so that by the time they were adults, they could take care of their own herds. Being a good horseman was of the utmost importance for these people.

Nikolas and all of his friends took to the saddle at an early age. They learned how to bridle a horse and get it ready for the long workday. They learned how to trot and gallop. They became proficient in backing up the horse and making it turn in any direction they desired without having to use the reins. Hanging on to the leather saddle with both hands, they could jump off and swing back onto the saddle, all while the horse was galloping. There were many more tricks and skills they practiced most of the week to become proficient.

As the boys and girls of this little nomadic community grew older, it became obvious that Nikolas was one of the best horsemen. He enjoyed riding his horse, and at the end of the day, he often came home and told his parents of the new tricks he had learned.

One day, a horrible storm raced across the steppe. In the distance, everybody could see the sky had turned black, and all could see, in the far distance, the lightning striking the earth. They could hear the thunder rolling across the wide-open fields of grass, and in the distance they could see a fire flaring up.

It was only a few days later that a small group of herdsmen and their families showed up at Nikolas and his family's community. They said they had lost a few tents in the fire. They were hoping to stay a while, until they could make new tents and move back to the part of the steppe from which they had come. It was a way of life among nomadic people to provide shelter for those in need, and so the people who lost their tents were welcomed into the community.

With the arrival of the small group of nomads, Nikolas and his friends were joined by a group of other boys and girls. Of course, they also had horses, and like Nikolas's group, they also practiced to become excellent horsemen. During the next few weeks, it became evident that Nikolas was no longer the top rider. Some of the boys and girls who recently joined their community matched Nikolas's skill in many areas, and in some particular horsemanship skills, his new peers surpassed him. Nikolas was disappointed. He enjoyed being the top rider, but now he had to share that honor with other boys and girls.

One morning, Nikolas told his parents that he did not want to go riding with the other kids. He just didn't feel good. He sat in his corner of the tent, rather angry. "My horse is just not doing what I want it to do," he said. So for the next several days Nikolas did not ride with the other kids. He tried to convince himself that it was his horse's fault.

One day, Nikolas took the horse out by himself. He wanted to test himself to see if he still had all the skills he had learned before. Much to his disappointment, he found out that his horse did not respond to his commands like it had done in the past. Somehow, the horse seemed to have forgotten some of the tricks Nikolas had taught him. Now he was very sad. He leaned up against the side of his horse and cried.

Suddenly, Nikolas heard a voice. At first he did not know where the voice came from, and he looked around. Then he heard the voice again. To his astonishment, it was his horse that spoke to him.

"What did you say? I did not understand you!" Nikolas said to the horse.

"I said, ride me!" said the horse.

"Why should I?" asked Nikolas. "We are not the best anymore! What's the use?"

For a while, the horse did not say anything. Nikolas stared at his horse. Then the horse spoke up.

"Remember when we were a good team and had a lot of fun learning new tricks together? Remember when we practiced all the time? If you don't ride me and we do not practice together, you will never be a good horseman and I will never be a good pony. And by the way, remember the trick where you stood up in the saddle, turned around, and sat back down? Nobody could do that trick as fast as us. And if you don't ride me, we will fall farther and farther behind."

That night, Nikolas lay in is bed for a long time, thinking about what his horse had said. He thought about it long and hard and said, "I'm not a coward. The horse is right. I don't have to be the best at all the tricks. As long as I'm enjoying myself and become a great horseman, I will be happy."

And so, the next morning, Nikolas saddled his horse and joined the other boys and girls. The horse was right; Nikolas became a great horseman.

The essential elements of the metaphor are these:

- The horsemanship tricks that Nikolas learned represent Oliver's academic accomplishments.

- The horse represents one's inner self, the subconscious—
  the part of oneself that carries on an inner conversation
  with oneself.

- Nikolas is reminded that by not practicing those tricks,
  he falls farther behind and that blaming someone else, or
  himself (the horse), is fruitless.

- He is reminded that to be good at something is very
  satisfying, but to be the best in everything is not necessary
  in order to become a well-rounded person.

The no-strategy approach simply addresses the obvious and presents a potential solution to an impasse.

When telling a story to a child, many parents rely on traditional fairy tales or rely on their own life experiences. While this approach has entertainment value and possibilities for a healing influence on the "troubled" child, the power of a customized story cannot be overrated. Creating the right story with the right strategy (or no strategy) possesses magical properties for a given listener. A customized story, more so than any other type, has the power to change perceptions and, thus, behavior. Moreover, the customized story is often long remembered. Why? Because the listener is invited—not forced—to extract meaning from it. Self-discovery is the best way to change behavior.

EPILOGUE

~~~~~~~~~~~~~~~~~~~~~~~~~~~~~~~~~~~~~~

a story for you—the reader

Centuries ago, in the Alpine region of Europe, lived a people who were herdsman of cattle and goats. They found that the high Alpine valleys, with their luscious meadows, were ideally suited for livestock. Which cow or goat would not want to feast on savory grass, herbs, and flowers?

During the long, harsh winter months, livestock was kept in the barn. Cows and goats were fed hay that families gathered during the summer months. On such long winter evenings, unable to do much work outside, families often gathered around small wood stoves for storytelling time. And so it was that Aeti, the grandfather, told a most-interesting tale to the small group huddled around the stove.

Once upon a time, there lived a farmer and his family in a country far, far away. Together, they plowed the fields and planted and garnered crops. In the summer they drove the cattle to the Alpine meadows where the milk was processed into cheese. Much of the cheese was traded for other goods needed during winter months, so the family was well supplied with what they needed.

One day, the family's youngest daughter, Anna, declared that she wanted to go out into the big, wide world to seek her fortune. "Be sure to take some goods and food with you, as you'll need it on your journey," said her father.

Anna packed a jug of water, a large loaf of bread, and a valuable silver coin in her knapsack. Kissing her parents good-bye, she went off to find her fortune.

Anna walked for a long time over hills, down country roads, and she crossed small streams. In the evening, having arrived at a large clearing in the woods, she decided that this was a great place to settle down for the night. She spread out her blanket under a tree and lay down. Looking up into the night sky, she was awestruck by the thousand lights that illuminated the meadow and trees around her. It was so bright that she noticed some of the lower branches of the tree above her had died, as the leaves had turned from green to brown. "What is wrong with you, Tree?" Anna asked.

"I don't get enough water," the tree answered. "I'm not strong enough for my roots to reach the brook nearby. I need more water for my roots to grow."

Anna, feeling bad for the tree, pulled the jug of water out of her knapsack and sprinkled its contents around the trunk. The tree said thank you, and Anna fell into a deep sleep. The next morning, Anna said good-bye to the tree and went on to seek her fortune.

Anna's journey took her over hills, through woods, and across rivers. After many weeks, she arrived at a small village. Looking for a place to stay for the night, she went from door to door, but nobody had a bed to spare. Finally, Anna came to the last house. She knocked on the door, and a boy stood before her. "How can I help you?" he asked.

"I'm looking for a bed to spend the night," Anna replied.

The boy invited her in. "I can offer you a bed, but unfortunately, I cannot offer you a meal. I have been sick, unable to work to earn money to purchase bread, and now I'm too weak to work."

Anna sat down, opened her knapsack, took out the loaf of bread, and invited the boy to eat as much as he could. "Thank you," the boy said, and Anna went to bed. The next morning, she rose early from a deep sleep and left to find her fortune.

A few days later, Anna came upon a large, half-plowed field where a single horse was hitched to a plow with his head hanging low. "What's the matter, Horse?" asked Anna.

"My name is Jacob," said the horse. He went on to explain that the sheriff had impounded Hans, the other horse that helped pull the plow. Jacob explained that without Hans, it was impossible to pull the plow and, therefore, the crops could not be planted. Anna inquired as to why Hans was impounded. Jacob explained that

Hans had eaten some grain of a different farmer's field. "He was very hungry," Jacob added.

"Maybe I can help," said Anna. She went down to the village and gave the sheriff her precious silver coin. "Will that coin purchase Hans's freedom?" she asked.

"Yes," said the sheriff.

Anna brought Hans to the field where Jacob stood in the harness of the plow. Without hesitation, Hans joined Jacob and together they plowed the field.

"Thank you," said the horses, and Anna went on her way to seek her fortune.

Anna traveled for many weeks, even months, but was unable to find her fortune. Discouraged, she decided to return home to her family. Retracing her way home, she came upon the place where she had met Hans and Jacob. The field was covered with a tall stand of grain. On the edge of the field stood a farmer with a sickle in his hand. He was in the process of mowing down row after row of grain. Anna smiled. With a bounce in her step, she continued her journey home.

She came upon the small village. Anna stopped in front of the house where she had met the boy and found shelter. The house looked clean and had a new coat of paint. "Where is the boy?" Anna asked a neighbor.

"He is at work," the neighbor replied. Anna smiled, both outwardly and within, as a warm feeling came over her.

A few days before she reached home, a rainstorm blew in from the north. Looking for shelter, she spotted a big tree with lots of leaves standing on the edge of a large clearing in the woods. Anna hurried across the clearing and stood under the tree. The big and healthy green leaves sheltered her from the rain. "I know you," said the tree. "The water you gave me many months ago allowed my roots to grow and tap into the nearby brook."

Anna's heart was aglow as she continued her homeward journey.

The listeners sat quietly in the dark until a young voice broke the silence, answering, "Her fortune was in helping others find theirs. And because of the good she spread along her quest for treasure, she was rewarded in her journey home by seeing the fruits of her kindness."

"Very good," said Aeti. "Now where will your journey take you?"